DISRUPTIVE
THINKING

DISRUPTIVE THINKING

A DARING STRATEGY TO CHANGE
HOW WE LIVE, LEAD, AND LOVE

T.D. JAKES
WITH NICK CHILES

NASHVILLE   NEW YORK

FaithWords
Hachette Book Group
1290 Avenue of the Americas, New York, NY 10104
faithwords.com
twitter.com/faithwords

First edition: May 2023

FaithWords is a division of Hachette Book Group, Inc. The FaithWords name and logo are trademarks of Hachette Book Group, Inc.

The publisher is not responsible for websites (or their content) that are not owned by the publisher.

The Mountain Is You, by Brianna Wiest. Copyright © 2020 Brianna Wiest. Reprinted with permission.

Unless otherwise indicated Bible verses are from the King James Version. Verses marked NIV are from the Holy Bible, New International Version®, NIV® Copyright © 1973, 1978, 1984, 2011 by Biblica, Inc.® Used by permission. All rights reserved worldwide. Scripture marked NKJV is taken from the New King James Version®. Copyright © 1982 by Thomas Nelson. Used by permission. All rights reserved.

The Hachette Speakers Bureau provides a wide range of authors for speaking events. To find out more, go to hachettespeakersbureau.com or email HachetteSpeakers@hbgusa.com.

FaithWords books may be purchased in bulk for business, educational, or promotional use. For information, please contact your local bookseller or the Hachette Book Group Special Markets Department at special.markets@hbgusa.com.

Library of Congress Control Number: 2023932139

Interior book design by Timothy Shaner, NightandDayDesign.biz

ISBNs: 9781546004004 (hardcover), 9781546004042 (ebook)

Printed in the United States of America

LSC-C

Printing 1, 2023

I would like to dedicate Disruptive Thinking *to John Hope Bryant, Janice Howroyd Bryant, and Payne Brown, who have been inspirational thought leaders and whose ability to navigate as change agents in this ever-changing environment have been instrumental in my own life! Furthermore, I want to dedicate this book to Bishop Sherman Watkins, who has been a father figure in my life for many years. A special thanks to Jan Miller, my literary agent, and Nick Chiles, whose literary expertise was invaluable in helping me achieve the deadlines and finesse my thoughts.*

Thanks also to Oscar Williams, Tristan Walker, Nona Jones, Keion Henderson, David Steward, Donna Richardson, Frederick Johnson, Christopher Lyons, Aaron Johnson and Anita Phillips for sharing their stories of disruptive thinking.

My final and most profound gratitude goes to my wife, Serita Jakes, and my five children, whose love and loyalty have given me the "why" to what I do every day! My love to each of you in your respective roles in my life!

CONTENTS

DISRUPTIVE THINKING

Your new life is going to cost you your old one.

It's going to cost you your comfort zone and your sense of direction.

It's going to cost you relationships and friends.

It's going to cost you being liked and understood.

It doesn't matter.

The people who are meant for you are going to meet you on the other side. You're going to build a new comfort zone around the things that actually move you forward. Instead of being liked, you're going to be loved. Instead of being understood, you're going to be seen.

All you're going to lose is what was built for a person you no longer are.

—Brianna Wiest, *The Mountain Is You: Transforming Self-Sabotage into Self-Mastery*

PREFACE

Can you remember that special morning when you were getting dressed for your first day of kindergarten—the apprehension, the terror, but also the undeniable excitement you felt? You were about to step into a completely new world, filled with people you had never encountered in your limited existence. Your most profound wish, the overwhelming goal that pressed down heavy on you like a weighted blanket, could be summarized with a simple question: *Will I fit in?*

Will I have on the right sneakers? Will I be wearing the right clothes? Will I look similar enough to everyone else that I won't stand out? Because what we desperately want is to be accepted. To be a part of the pack. To belong.

What fascinates me about that moment is how much that early question continues to dominate our thinking for the rest of our lives. In so many respects, on so many levels, that query shapes the way we live. It never fully goes away. Recently, I was invited to the Kennedy Center Honors award ceremony at the Opera House in Washington, DC. It's a lovely, special evening where luminaries gather in sartorial splendor to celebrate legends of stage and screen. I'm talking extreme black tie, fancy stuff. I made sure I had on my spiffiest tuxedo, so that no one would look askance at me and wonder, *What in the world could Jakes have been thinking?* No, I had to look the part—which in this case meant looking like every other guy in the room.

Whether it's corporate America, church, or school, in so many settings our greatest desire is to not stand out. To be homogeneous with the environment in which we find ourselves. When we step outside of our homes, we participate in a social contract that we all implicitly sign, whether we realize it or not. Behave as everyone else behaves. Dress like the rest of us. Don't attract too much notice. We know that our ability to fit in will sometimes determine whether we get the promotion, whether we get accepted into the sorority—or the gang. And we will do whatever we have to do—get the grades, score the touchdowns, apply the makeup, buy the sneakers, steal the sneakers—to fit into that group we covet.

However, there is a hidden truth embedded inside this phenomenon. The people who are written into the history books, who make the hall of fame, who unearth world-changing discoveries, who become the exceptional among us, are not the ones who fit in. They are the disrupters who decided they no longer cared about fitting in. They were seeking something else—something they determined was more important than being accepted.

As a society, we have become conditioned to sit in our lives, to accept our circumstances—however unpleasant they may be—while we wait for someone to come along and save us. As we watched television, flocked to the movies, read the newspaper, we were trained to think that if our life went askew, someone would save us. In my day it was Superman, Batman, and the Lone Ranger. Today, it's Wakanda and the Black Panther. And there are also the real-life heroes, like John F. Kennedy, Martin Luther King Jr., Jesse Jackson, Nelson Mandela, and Barack Obama. We even put their pictures up on the wall, as if to give them a better vantage point to bear witness to our suffering need. If only we were a little more patient, they would rescue us from our circumstances.

Why do we need saving? Sometimes it's because of the bad choices of someone else, such as a parent, spouse, or particularly malicious boss. But more times than not it's because of the choices we make ourselves. In physiological terms, perhaps our prefrontal cortex—the area of the brain that allows us to foresee possible implications for our actions and stop us from impulsive mistakes—didn't activate with enough force to stop us from making the kinds of decisions that would put us in precarious situations that required rescue.

The older we get, the longer we live, the more we realize that we are born looking like our parents, but we die looking like our decisions.

As you embark with me on this journey exploring the power and necessity of disruptive thinking, you should know that I had in mind both the people who are willing to let their hair down and embrace disruption, like Rapunzel, and the people waiting for Batman or the Black Panther to hit the ground and vanquish our bad decisions.

What we all eventually begin to realize is that no one's coming. As the Bible wisely states in Proverbs 23:7, "For as he thinketh in his heart, so is he." The mind and the body collaborate to produce the energy, the fuel, the fortitude to change our lives. But will we concede? Will we allow our brain's amygdala—the structure in the brain's temporal lobe that attaches emotional significance to memories—to take our memories and have them processed in a way that fuels our frontal lobe decisions? Will we acquiesce to blending in and forgo the opportunity to be delivered, changed, altered? Will we succumb to the abyss of living in regret over the choices we did not make?

I believe that once we realize that no one is coming, the onus is upon us to produce the energy to fight or to flee (or give in to fear and freeze). What makes one person fight and another one run or freeze?

A big part of our response mechanism is connected to the way we store our experiences as memories. Are our memories stashed away in a toxic brew that creates fears and phobias? Dealing with those sometimes requires therapy to help us experience those memories with less trauma, thus allowing us to make choices without activating the adrenaline rush to fight or flee or giving in to the fear and freezing. If we don't find a way to process those memories in a positive way, it will lead us to stress, anxiety, and bad decisions. In Romans 12:2, the Bible describes it as "transformed by the renewing of the mind" (NIV)—but a new spirit, even when regenerated, still has to declutter the way we process what happened in our lives. Most of us just move the memories into the attic of our minds until the smell of the debris contaminates the entire house.

One of the most disruptive thinkers in the Bible was the risk-taking, outspoken, outlandish, nonconforming apostle Peter. Though the former fisherman is less intellectual, throughout the Bible he is the quickest to be disruptive—sometimes inappropriately. Why does he leave the safety of the boat and the other eleven disciples to walk on water toward Jesus with only one word of permission: "Come" (Matt. 14:22–33)? Why does he take out his sword and cut off the ear of a Roman soldier, knowing that they're outnumbered (John 18:10)? Why does Peter alone break the silence and speak up when Jesus asks, "Who do you say I am?" with the response "You are the Messiah, the Son of the living God" (Matt. 16:15–16 NIV)? Why on the day of Pentecost is Peter chosen to deliver the inaugural address of a new era (Acts 2:14–41)? Because he's a disrupter.

In the absence of any superheroes, living or fictitious, in the absence of world-changing leaders, the onus for change rests on us. We are the people, the leaders, and the superheroes we've been waiting for.

This book is about those of us who are willing to change our lives, rather than to live in the regrets of what if . . . what might have . . . what should have happened. It is about those of us willing to change the plight of our community, our office, our church, our own behavior. If you're not willing to disrupt the status quo, if you're more comfortable running with the herd, the thrust of this book might not include you. But if there is a drive inside of you that suspects you might have a better life, a better love, a better marriage, a better career, then I suggest to you that as a man thinketh in his heart, you can think your way into disruption without being destructive—with the lasting intent of changing your world, in your own lifetime.

The reason for writing this book at this time is because our society seems to be headed for a cataclysmic collision of biblical proportions. The clanging dissonance of violence, anger, fear, and political dissolution threatens to suffocate us all. I don't see any lights in the sky; I don't see any superheroes flying through the air in automated cars like in Wakanda. I don't see anyone coming to save us but us.

It starts not with burnings and marching and protests and scaling the White House walls; it starts in the privacy of our own head—which incidentally is the final frontier of true privacy. The privacy of our thoughts is the only safe space we have left—a space that cannot be hacked, invaded, or surveilled. It is the sole remaining place where we have true freedom to think for ourselves. But we must be aware that people are after us every day to rob us—not of our jewelry, watches, cars, or houses. No, they are trying to rob us of our opinion. We have to fight for it, contest for it, wrestle for it, because it is the catalyst for every true reformative act that has ever happened in history. The revolutionary reveries of our brain is where all transformation starts.

I want you to know that disruptive thinking is within your reach. And if you use your adrenaline for the courage to fight or flee and use your brain to decide which one is appropriate at the particular time—fight, flee, or freeze—it is your choice, and your choice alone.

But if you're afraid of disruption, if you succumb to peer pressure, if you're not willing to stand out, then you will die looking like that decision. You can't be disruptive if you idolize conformists. You can't be disruptive and conformist at the same time; you have to forsake one for the other. The apostle Peter had to make a decision: Do I stay on the boat with my comrades, where it's safe, or do I disrupt this whole thing and walk out on the water? Yes, he got in trouble on the water when he got distracted and fearful and momentarily lost his faith; he almost drowned and had to be saved by Jesus. But he's the only apostle who can ever say he got to walk on water. Sometimes the risk is worth the reward.

Mahatma Gandhi, Nelson Mandela, Martin Luther King Jr., and John Lewis all decided the risk was worth the reward. The question for us is whether there is something inside of us that suspects we could be more than our environment suggests—maybe a pull, a tug, a yank, a push. In my case, there was a feeling I couldn't put my finger on that kept haunting me, telling me I could live a better life in spite of my flaws, my environment, my circumstances, my insecurities, my intimidation. None of those invisible fences were strong enough to keep me from taking the job, accepting the assignment. Like Esther, I told myself, if I perish, then I perish. But I'm going.

At the end of our journey together dissecting the crux of disruptive thinking, I will offer to you a collection of eleven moving testimonials from individuals I have chosen because of their extraordinary examples of disruption. From a corporate titan to a cutting-edge barber, from a fearless entrepreneur to a trauma therapist, from a tech leader to a best-selling author, these are trendsetters who have used disruptive thinking to outrun the herd. I wanted them to go on record and be the living epistles that authenticate the validity of what you will read in these pages. They are your disciples. All that you will digest, they have done. So, the next chapter, the next story, will be on you.

Welcome to disruptive thinking.

ONE

WHAT IS DISRUPTIVE THINKING?

When I was eleven, I watched my father waste away before my eyes.

At six feet and 280 pounds, Ernest Jakes loomed as large as the West Virginia mountains that surrounded our home. When he stepped into a room, the shadows receded in resignation, the molecules launched their own frenzied praise dance. From his barrel chest emerged a booming baritone whose bottom I felt in my bones. I once saw him get out of the car, wade into the snow to lift a car that was stuck, and tell the driver to hit the gas to get back on the road.

But on the inside, the state of his kidneys belied his bulging biceps and triceps. At the age of thirty-eight, Ernest Jakes suffered debilitating kidney failure. The kidneys could no longer go it alone. They would need our help.

And my life would never be the same.

I watched his body slowly wither away. He went from 280 pounds to 130 pounds. His muscular thighs sagged like a ninety-year-old man shirtless on the beach. He went from driving heavy-duty equipment and steering loaded trucks to being pushed in a wheelchair. The Incredible Hulk became Pee-wee Herman. It was the most distressing sight I have ever witnessed.

Disruption kicked down the door and made itself at home in the Jakes household. Any sense of normalcy I previously enjoyed became a distant memory. For a year after his kidney failure, I would help my mother load my weakening dad into the car to make the four-hour drive to Cleveland from our home in Charleston, West Virginia. In 1968, the Cleveland Clinic was the closest place to Charleston to get dialysis treatment. Once a week, we had to trek across the Midwest to keep him alive.

At age eleven, I had to step into the ill-fitting shoes of an adult. After school, I boarded a bus to head to my father's offices to make sure the buildings were locked and the checks got delivered to the fifty-two people he employed in his janitorial company. My older brother was gone, so it fell on me. My father trusted me to do what needed to be done to help keep his business afloat. I was not going to disappoint him.

My father's life-changing diagnosis came just as the family's fortunes were brightening. We were like the Jeffersons would be nearly a decade later, about to move on up to the east side. We had just moved into a much bigger house, one that allowed me and my two siblings finally to have our own rooms. Before the move, we lived at the end of a dirt road on Page Street, in a community called Vandelia in the suburbs of Charleston. Vandelia was split into the white neighborhood and the "colored" neighborhood. The five of us made do in a two-bedroom house that was held up in the rear by four-by-four-inch posts wedged into the side of the hill. We didn't know we were poor, because everybody was poor. We didn't have air-conditioning. We didn't have grass in the front yard. We didn't have a doorbell. But we had each other. No, we weren't a perfect family, and we had our fair share of dysfunction. Still, there was a certain joy and peace.

My father did everything his hands and mind could conceive to feed us—selling fish door-to-door when I was a little boy, hawking a variety of household goods to the surrounding community, and finally starting a janitorial service that at its height had fifty-two employees and ten trucks working across the state. We moved into our new home, which seemed enormous to us at about three thousand square feet. We had a lovely porch with a white wrought-iron railing that was formed into the shape of a twisty metal grapevine. We had a patio, a carpeted basement, a laundry room, knotty pine wood paneling on the walls, and air-conditioning. For a family that grew up in a two-bedroom house hanging off a cliff, it was amazing. In the words of the song Whitney Houston made popular, "Didn't we almost have it all?"

I was the baby of the family, protected and acutely treasured as I was sandwiched between two dead babies. My mother birthed five children, but only three survived. The child before me died nameless in her womb. The one after me, my sister Marionette, was a stillborn whose body is buried in a cemetery in Charleston. And though I too was once gravely ill as a toddler, I survived. Ours was a household where fun hovered in the air, boosted by each of us in our own way. When Mom and Dad hit the town for date nights, they would head to the Shoney's, our idea of haute cuisine. As she savored her favorite shrimp dinner, my mother always made sure to smuggle rolls in her pocketbook to bring back to us. I would become intoxicated by the faint fragrance of the shrimp that still lingered on the bread—I still love shrimp more than a half century later because of that memory.

My mother taught us all to read and write before our feet ever entered a schoolroom. We all took classical piano lessons—and all complained about taking classical piano lessons. My sister Jacqueline was the only one who had real talent. I can still hear her fingers glide across the keys when relatives or friends came around. We entertained ourselves with homemade talent shows. Once I even saw my mother and father dance. It was a sight I never forgot. They seldom showed affection publicly. I was delighted to see them dancing and not bickering.

It was a joyful time and place. Until it wasn't. Now our provider needed provision. I learned quickly that we are all one event away from calamity.

After a year of weekly treks to Cleveland, we had a dialysis machine installed in our house. The laundry room became the dialysis room—the hospital room. It contained a bed and the rather large dialysis machine. At five feet long and two and a half feet wide, the machine was an unusual sight in an American home in 1968. On the top of the machine was a strange plastic compartment through which blood ran as it was being purified. There were many gauges, dials, and knobs. A bottle hung from the top like an IV, flowing into the shunt in my father's arm. The machine had an alarm that sounded loud and ominous if something went wrong. I learned how to operate every detail of the machine. In fact, the first picture of me that ever appeared in a newspaper, *The Charleston Gazette*, showed me standing next to the machine alongside my mother as we watched over my dad getting his twice-weekly treatment. His narrow, strained face looked to me like the face of a stranger.

Everything that was normal about my life was gone. I no longer had time to be a child. I didn't have time to be scared when I boarded the bus and headed to his business. I had to go make decisions and be responsible and come back to report to him on everything that had happened. While my friends on the block were playing football and basketball and riding bicycles, I was assuming the responsibilities of a grown man. The sports part wasn't much of a loss to me, because I never did have any sports inclination or abilities. I couldn't play outside with them, but I could change the membranes in the kidney machine, wrap up a shunt, clean up blood, and prime the machine.

In other words, I learned to handle disruption. Disruptive thinking became second nature to me. It became my normal. It has been said that God will promote you to the level of your tolerance of pain. Well, I guess I was being groomed by tragedy, disruption, and responsibility to handle my life now as a direct result of my life then.

It has been said that hard times produce strong leaders, and good times produce weak leaders. I've seen that play out in my own life. As I began to think about the primacy of disruptive thinking to our world and the elements that forge disruptive thinkers, like a chemist titrating in the lab, I kept coming back to my early days and their impact on my evolution. Disruptive thinking is not often something we're drawn to, it is usually part of our survival mechanism in response to circumstances thrust upon us. We have to find a way to get it done when traditional methods don't work, when normalcy is shattered. These disruptions were terribly painful to me, but they led to powerful outcomes.

One of the most disruptive moments of my childhood came when I was thirteen. We were about two years into the home dialysis when something went wrong with the dialysis machine. I can still hear that alarm ringing out across the household that night, reaching deep inside each of us and cranking up the panic switch. We needed to get my dad to the hospital as soon as possible. I was carrying metal pans in case he threw up in the car and blankets to ward off the frigid West Virginia winter.

As we moved outside and onto the front porch, my father grabbed hold of the wrought-iron railing and wouldn't let go. He didn't want to go to the hospital.

"Please, let me die," he said, his voice weak, pleading. "Let me die."

I was a child, hearing my father say he wanted to die. He didn't want to fight anymore. He didn't want to be helpless anymore. He didn't want to be in a wheelchair anymore, or to have them punching any more holes in his stomach for proposed feeding tubes. He was a relatively young man who had lost his muscles, his barrel chest, his virility. Everything that he was proud of. He just wanted it all to end. He didn't think he had anything left to live for.

I dropped everything from my arms and I leaped forward, toward his fingers. One by one, I pried his fingers from the railing, as he cried and protested. I didn't say it, but one devastating thought dropped into my head.

Live for me, Dad. Live for me.

Three years later, he was gone. He finally got his wish.

All of us who came of age in the 1960s lived in a time of disruption. We know what it looks like to have chaos swirling around us, threatening to annihilate us as a society. We saw the buildings that had signs designating them as fallout shelters in case we were bombed. We saw the headlines reporting on the death tolls in Vietnam as war protests flowed through the streets. We saw signs on houses warning you to stay away because there was tuberculosis inside. Diseases were still running amok as penicillin became more widely available. The president had been shot dead in full view of the nation, something we hadn't seen in a hundred years. Racial tensions were off the charts, as we watched Mahalia Jackson in *Imitation of Life*, a film that delved into the painful consequences of a fair-skinned Black woman passing as white. There were still occasional lynchings in the South. Medgar Evers was murdered. The four charred bodies of beautiful young girls were seen on the six o'clock news, carried from the Sixteenth Street Baptist Church. Addie Mae Collins, Cynthia Wesley, Denise McNair, and Carole Robertson would never come home for Sunday dinner. And Black people and some white people began to understand that this was the inflection point. Or was it?

Everywhere we turned during those years, we saw what felt like impending doom. But from that doom came great artistic creativity. Bras were burning. Woodstock was grooving. Jimi Hendrix was jamming. British bands like the Beatles were invading American culture. I can still see white go-go boots, elephant leg pants with platform shoes. Fashion and fire. Cassius Clay had converted to Islam and now Muhammad Ali was introduced to a traumatized country. The music played in symphonic syncopation as strobe lights twinkled and disco lights flashed. Jitterbug and hot combs had transformed to afros and assassinations. It was all happening simultaneously. New forms of business were birthed as the country transitioned from the agricultural age. The migration to the Northern states continued. The industrial age would eventually segue to technology in Silicon Valley and information would move from color TVs to tweets and posts on Facebook. We emerged from those frightening times undaunted, though scarred—and many of those scars still remain.

But the point is that our current strife—social justice, racism, war, social upheaval, disease—all feels disturbingly familiar. We've seen this movie before. From Emmett Till to George Floyd. From Vietnam to Ukraine. From the resignation of President Nixon to the impeachment of President Trump. These eyes have seen a lot.

How does disruption affect the way we think, how we see the world and its possibilities? We emerged from that previous era of enormous disruption with untold discoveries, transformative businesses, earth-shaking music and art and literature. We are now at a similar inflection point as a society, as a global community. How are we going to take the disruption we are seeing and use it as an opportunity to create radical change? How can we become disruptive thinkers at a time when the vortex of decadence threatens the very existence of our society?

What it all comes down to is this: How do we respond to trouble?

How do we respond to calamity and chaos? Will we be so orthodox in our thinking that we don't explore options beyond the veil of human acceptance—or will we jump the fence? Will we find a way to thrive in an environment that is not conducive to normalcy?

One of the most transformative figures of our time is a classic example of a disruptive thinker: Elon Musk. While the debate over the existence of global warming and climate change raged—and somehow continues to rage—with volleys sent back and forth between the scientists and the politicians, Musk took an untrodden path. He knew America thrived on capitalism above everything else, so he leaned into innovation and built electric cars that changed the game—making staggering amounts of money in the process. I'm not glamorizing who he is, because I don't know him at all, but I have been struck by the saliency and power of his disruptive thinking. In the midst of an endless debate, he cut through it and appealed to the base nature of our capitalistic society. When they tried to shut him out of the traditional channels used by car manufacturers, Musk found a way around the system. Through his groundbreaking technology, he has become incredibly prosperous as the progenitor of innovation that disrupted everything. Now everybody's making electric cars and semi-electric cars.

Disrupters don't take sides; they take over.

Musk didn't join the argument over climate change, he just went to the solution. He knew that money would override the debate. When Americans were fuming over rising gas prices in early 2022, I didn't understand the distress. My primary car is a Telsa, so I didn't feel that pain. I just plugged my car in at night, unplugged it in the morning, and took off.

Every period of chaos brings with it a gift—an opportunity to disrupt the chaos by providing a solution rather than joining the debate. Disruptive thinking isn't about picking a side in the argument; it's about stepping past the argument toward a solution.

If we sift through American history, we see that the major purveyors of radical change were disruptive thinkers. As Abraham Lincoln rose to the American presidency, American society never seriously contemplated ending slavery. Slavery was too lucrative to let morality, justice, and human decency enter the equation. Slavery was the economic engine that fueled America and enabled the nation to reach a point where it could even contemplate independence from England. Lincoln stepped into the presidency and yanked out the rug from racism and economic empowerment—in the process destroying the net worth of millionaires in the South, because Black people were considered assets to the estate. Because of the secession of the Southern states, Lincoln was able to create a national banking system, issuing banknotes called greenbacks that looked alike and were distributed through chartered national banks—replacing the chaotic system of hundreds of private banks issuing their own unique banknotes. He also created the first ever national income tax to bring much-needed funds into the nation's coffers.

Lincoln was hated by many for his efforts, and ultimately killed, which brings me to a crucial point about the controversial nature of disrupters. They are often appreciated only after their funerals.

After all, who was more disruptive than Jesus?

He came into a society where there were conflicts raging between the Greeks and the Jews and between the Samaritans and the Jews. But Jesus ends up not taking sides—He ends up taking over with a disruptive idea of something called a church that emerged out of the conflict. It wasn't orthodox so the priests hated Him. It wasn't political so the Romans feared Him. It wasn't Samaritan so they had no dealings with Him. And yet He found the path.

Disruptive thinking is about finding a solution and a path toward it, rather than joining a gang and continuing a debate that might outlive you. The debate still rages over the biblical question "Who is my neighbor?" In Luke 10, when a lawyer asks Jesus, "Who is my neighbor?" Jesus responds by telling the parable of the Good Samaritan who cares for the man left half-dead by robbers by the side of the road. When He told the story, Jesus knew that the Jews didn't deal with the Samaritans. They had the same kind of racial dynamics and theological dynamics that we have today. Jesus makes a hero out of the character the Jews would have seen as the villain, then he asks the lawyer, "Who is your neighbor?" That's totally disruptive. To me, Jesus was one of the most nonreligious people we've ever seen. He disrupted religious people.

If we look at some of the people who did groundbreaking things in music and art, we see how they did so by being disruptive. Lena Horne is celebrated for her beauty and grace, but she was constantly fighting against injustice during her career. She sued restaurants and theaters for discriminating against her as she performed across the country. She filed a complaint after she entertained troops at Fort Riley, Kansas, during World War II and saw that the Black soldiers had to sit in the back—behind the German POWs. She financed her own travel to entertain Black troops when MGM Studios pulled her off its tour. She was a disrupter.

So was the great Mahalia Jackson. While she is revered as the most successful and popular gospel music artist of all time, she wasn't warmly received in all circles. A lot of churches refused to let her sing because she was putting a beat behind traditional gospel songs, and they said she was singing honky-tonk or the blues. Yet she persisted as a disruptive force, remaking gospel music in the process and influencing generations of singers who followed her. When she died in 1972, her estate had a value of $1 million (the equivalent of almost $7 million today)—at a time when the words *Black* and *million* almost never appeared in the same sentence.

If you have the courage to turn the page and continue to read, know that the pathway forward may be painful. At times, it may even be bloody. But if you're going to make it to the halls of transformative success and change the world, it's going to require disruptive thinking.

It took me many years to consider the ways in which the disruption I experienced early in my life, personally and societally, left a positive deposit on me. I was immersed so long in the pain that for the longest time I couldn't see the power. Often, it's not what you're running to but what you're running from that pushes you beyond the pale of normalcy. The urgency of moving erratically away from sheer terror can produce greatness. Who knows if Oprah Winfrey would have become the disruptive force she ultimately became if not for the horrific trials of child abuse and rape she suffered in her early years. Would Maya Angelou have become such an exceptional chronicler of the human condition without the trauma and abuse she suffered?

What's in you from early trauma often causes your pace to be quicker than that of others who are less stimulated to go forward. Fear is what motivated Noah to build an ark after God told him He would destroy all the people on earth because of their wickedness. However, there comes a point when you have to fire your board of directors—meaning that what brought you here won't take you there. You can't keep running all your life. You have to settle those old accounts and be motivated by something other than what you're running from. There's a transition point where the method may be baked in but the motivation must change.

For me that transition has been a long process. The un-settled feelings of my childhood and around my father's death made me feel very unsafe. Poverty made me feel very unsafe. Being Black made me feel very unsafe. At some point during my journey, I looked around, and I started to feel safe. I'm still not sure I'm totally safe, but I'm safer than I was. However, now the feeling and the worry gets transferred to my children: are they safe?

For marginalized peoples in a society, that question likely never fully dissipates. Do you ever feel safe? Should you feel safe? And when you do, you fight survivor's guilt—why you and not the guy on the corner clearly down on his luck?

As we try to move to safety for ourselves and our children and grandchildren, we reach a point where we worry about whether we have made things *too* safe for them. We hope that our incessant need to make things better for them didn't make them less capable human beings, less able to withstand the trials that will come their way because they didn't experience any disruption growing up.

A lot of the things we debate about today as a society are the luxuries of not having a crisis. When the Twin Towers were attacked on 9/11, the country was in the middle of acrimonious political debate. But the Clintons and the Bushes gathered in the same sanctuary, singing and praying together. Black people and white people were all aligned. All of a sudden a greater threat canceled out all other threats. As a society, we fight now about things that don't really matter because these are the luxuries of not being at war. We create internal skirmishes about masks and vaccines, additional bathrooms to accommodate emerging sexual revolutions. Is now the time for a new political party? All these things and more are the debates we can afford because of the absence of war, terrorist attacks, a hack in our electrical grids, or the collapse of our already failing infrastructure.

But those of us born under attack have to redefine the purpose of our lives and convert that early energy into something useful. I grew up in West Virginia and married a woman whose family worked in the coal mines. She's literally a coal miner's daughter—it's not just a song for me. Anybody who came out of the coal fields will tell you that every time you turn on a light switch you should remember them because what's black coming out of the mines looks white with light from electricity. How do you convert the dark places into light? That is the residue of being around and surviving disruption. The residue is the thought process that stays with you—it's really a gift to you that redefines what you call trouble that you're willing to worry about and changes your stress levels. A friend of mine says, "God will promote you to the level of your tolerance of pain." Your tolerance of pain is changed, like the frog in the boiling water, by how much pain accrues while you're in a state that you think of as normal. The frog gets used to the slowly heating water, so he still sees it as normal when it begins to boil—but drop another frog in the boiling water and he's going to have a problem.

If I wanted to kill you, to utterly destroy you, I would hand you my life and my responsibilities and adversities, my family, the companies I manage, the financial challenges of entrepreneurship, or even just the management of our church. It would kill you because the water didn't heat up slowly for you.

I began to feel a slight degree of safety when I felt my staff grow and my experience increase. I had a sense of security. I know that things like freedom, rights, equity, and a path forward can be threatened by our passivity toward change. When it gets threatened, my default is disruptive thinking. My way of fighting for social justice is to teach and model entrepreneurship and fight for job placement and rehabilitation for the incarcerated. You must find something that's organic to who you are and that's solution-oriented, because we either scream at the darkness or we light a candle. I don't think screaming at the darkness always works—it doesn't always change things.

My default has become that I'm happy only when I'm a little intimidated. It makes me careful and thoughtful, investigative and collaborative. I have to have a giant to kill, something to fight. And I need somebody in my life to tell me when to stop. Balance comes with the humility of knowing what you're not good at doing. Accessorize your limitations by developing relationships with people whose talent complements your limitations.

You must come in at the door. If you pull up to a house, you don't look for the window, but the door. When pursuing your place in the world, you must come in at the door. That's the place of entry into the discovery of what's inside the opportunity and, more importantly, what's inside of you. However, most sane people don't spend the day at the door.

Music was where I began to enter my future. But it was not my end. Once I got past the threshold—which some people never do—it led to ministry. Ministry led to marketplace, film, television, real estate development, philanthropy—and I'm still evolving. You only stop living when you stop evolving. That's when your search for a life of learning ends. The insatiable thirst for learning is quenched the moment you stop evolving. Music and ministry are great. I've done that for years, but I didn't get stuck at the point of entry. Doors lead to larger rooms. You can't get to the many rooms if you're stuck at the door.

Every great house has many doors, if you have the courage and the will to tour the house. You must get beyond the phase one level of just finding something you can authentically do. Because where you start may not be where you finish.

Several years before I established the Potter's House, I founded TDJ Enterprises. It is a social impact holding company, an LLP incorporated as an S corporation solely so that I could continue to explore my entrepreneurial side while following my ecclesiastical calling to serve. My for-profit company gave me the ability to tour the country doing plays and selling memorabilia and music from the gospel plays. I began to develop relationships in the entertainment space and the business space, and in the process I learned a little about promotions, productions, and plays. It was through that company that I started my literary career and radio show, *Empowering Moments*, which was featured on Radio One through a revenue sharing model. Eventually the plays would be the conduit that led to producing films.

At some point I realized that the notion of bi-vocationally extending my career was rooted in the legacy of my father the entrepreneur and deepened by the fact that in my early years as a pastor of an extremely small church in Montgomery, West Virginia, I needed a full-time job to survive. So, I've always traveled down parallel lanes. While I was in the embryonic stages of ministry and business, nobody was paying much attention to the model—though it was building an economic foothold on a better future for me and my family and, more importantly, was a model for many others to explore more for their development and ability to contribute from a larger space.

However, as I became more prominent, society found it quite difficult to describe my disruptive thinking, because people desperately need to describe you by comparisons. *Time* magazine put me on the cover in September 2001 (the week after 9/11) as "America's Best Preacher" and asked in a bold headline, "Is This Man the Next Billy Graham?" While the comparison was complimentary, it didn't fully describe the model. I knew that my choices to travel in both ministry and marketplace lanes disrupted the sensibilities of organized religion as well as outsiders. Later on, I realized that the late Billy Graham was himself more than a renowned evangelist. He would found the Billy Graham Evangelistic Association, which would diversify his brand, produce films, author books, and develop philanthropy; it continues to exist through his son Franklin and his grandson Will. Graham did all of this without ever being labeled a prosperity preacher.

That's not to say he or I were without detractors. But if you step off the beaten path, expect some thorns and briars. Initially it's quite natural to want to clear up any and all misperceptions about you. However, you have to eventually decide who you're trying to impact— your detractors or the world?

You can't be a disruptive thinker while trying to negotiate peace settlements with people who want to define you by their description of you. Everyone who met me as a musician struggled to see me as a minister. Everyone who met me as a minister struggled to see me as an entrepreneur. Their snide remarks were born out of their discomfort with my mobility. I couldn't afford to alter my definition of success to make my observers comfortable. Sooner or later a decision has to be reached that will set the tone for your lifelong priorities. Should you decide to be bold enough to be a drum major of a paradigm shift, you can't forever litigate the opinions of those who call fouls and plays from the bleachers. Whew! That took a while for me to learn. The sting of those you stun leaves deep welts. If you're not careful, you'll not fulfill your purpose in pursuit of their acceptance. Simply stated, are you willing to compromise your uniqueness for their camaraderie?

Standing up requires standing out. Sometimes limping, other times leaping, I climbed the literary ladder. I won Grammys, NAACP Image Awards, and several awards for our Texas Offenders Reentry Initiative. I won a Santa Barbara Film Festival award and BET awards, became the first clergyperson to be appointed to the executive board of the Dallas Regional Chamber of Commerce, graced the cover of the *Wall Street Journal*, currently sit on the governor's board for the Dallas Symphony Orchestra, and much more. That's not taking a deep plunge into the pool of grandiosity. Instead, it is meant to level set what can be expected when one is willing to be disruptive in order to become more effective.

TWO

WHY DO WE NEED DISRUPTIVE THINKING NOW?

What does desolation look like?

Increasingly, it looks like America.

We are seeing a loud splintering of the social arrangement that has sustained Americans for generations—the belief that hard work will bring you and yours the stability we all crave. Get a good enough job, go to work every day, watch over your kids, and America will smile down upon you.

For far too many Americans, that's not happening anymore. Their country now is more likely to offer them a frown than a smile. Maybe even a grimace.

Wealth inequality has become the social kindling of the twenty-first century, crackling underneath us, awaiting a spark to ignite either a destructive national conflagration or a beneficent societal transformation.

Wade into the numbers chronicling the shift in American wealth over the past half century and you find yourself reading the transcript of the implosion of the American experiment—and perhaps the detonating fuse for a national explosion.

As recently as 1965, the typical CEO of an American company made twenty times the salary of their average worker. By 2021, that number had soared to an average of 399 times more than the average worker, according to an Economic Policy Institute report. CEOs earned an average of $15.6 million in 2021.[1] To make it worse, CEO salaries continue to climb—an analysis by Compensation Advisory Partners found they shot up by 19 percent in 2021.[2] Wait a minute, wasn't that during the pandemic, when small businesses were closing and there was a national moratorium placed on evictions for masses of displaced workers? When there were closed restaurants and company layoffs? The workers who were able to have a job at all were flatlined. Worker salaries? They didn't even increase enough to keep up with inflation. That's painful enough on paper, but with these staggering gaps rank-and-file workers can't help but wonder: Am I working for my family—or my boss's yacht? Am I staying late for me—or the stockholders and the top 5 percent?

In 2020, the richest of the rich—the top 5 percent of the population—earned 23 percent of all US income, according to census numbers. The top 20 percent earned 52.2 percent of all income.[3] The employers of those struggling at the bottom typically offer no health insurance, no sick days, no pension plans. Those workers can't take off if they get sick, and they can't afford medicine—or to take their kid to the dentist. There are few things more unsettling, more enraging.

Not surprisingly, the picture gets even uglier when you divide the population by race. A quarter of all Black households have zero or negative net worth—only 10 percent of white families are that poor, according to the Economic Policy Institute. Black families have just $5.04 in net worth for every $100 held by white families.[4]

Between 1983 and 2013, white households saw their wealth increase by 14 percent while Black households saw their wealth *decline* by 75 percent.[5] Staggering. Between 2005 and 2015, the home ownership rates for Black households steadily declined. That is the very epitome of what it means to fall further behind.

Generations of grueling work to pull up Black households to a standard of living that might be described as minimally bearable have not borne fruit. Mobility is nonexistent. Has all the toil been in vain? The astute work of Princeton economist Ellora Derenoncourt revealed that there has been no progress in closing the wealth gap since 1950—and in fact since the 1980s the gap has been widening. Black households had more movement in the decades after enslavement.[6]

Economists have fingered a major reason for this discrepancy: inherited wealth. White adults are more than twice as likely as Black and Latino households to get significant financial help from parents and other elders, according to a 2022 poll by NPR, the Robert Wood Johnson Foundation, and the Harvard T.H. Chan School of Public Health.[7]

"You have Black Americans who are doing everything they were told is right and not getting ahead," Dorothy Brown, a Georgetown tax law professor, told NPR. "And they're scratching their heads wondering, 'How come I'm not doing better than I am? How come I'm not doing better than the guy in the cubicle next to me?'"[8]

Thirty-eight percent of white adults reported to pollsters that they had gotten at least $10,000 in gifts or loans from a parent or older relative, while just 14 percent of Black adults report the same (those numbers are 16 percent for Latinos and 19 percent for Native Americans), according to the NPR poll. In fact, for Black adults, Brown points out, generational wealth transfer is more likely to work in the reverse—children sending money to their parents, whose income over generations has steadily declined.

However, the winds of despair in recent years have swept into communities that have seldom felt their chill. While the top 1 percent of wage earners in the US saw their income increase by 229 percent between 1979 and 2019, skilled rural men have not seen their earnings change in fifty years.[9] Reports show that rural children are more likely than urban children to be poor, and they are also more likely to live in areas with high rates of poverty—poor families in poor communities. These rural areas have lower rates of educational attainment than urban areas, higher shares of single-mother-led families, and higher shares of work in service industries. These aren't just Black and brown communities, though they are the pictures that make the news. Americans in general are suffering from a hemorrhaging middle-class economy.

In other words, poverty and despair are being felt across America in a wide variety of communities, by Americans with a wide variety of skin tones. This pain has been showing up in recent years in the death rates of Americans. While the age-adjusted death rates in both rural and urban areas have been falling, the rates have risen among white rural residents between ages twenty-five and sixty-four.[10] Researchers have been describing the trend as "deaths of despair"—increases in deaths from drug and alcohol abuse, suicide, chronic liver diseases, and cirrhosis. In fact, the difference in rural and urban death rates tripled over the past twenty years, mostly due to deaths among middle-aged white men and women—who now account for a third of all US suicides.

America is literally dying on the vines. If ever there was a time for disruption, this is it.

Political scientists wondered how so many Americans could vote for both Barack Obama and Donald Trump, but economists knew the answer: They were searching for change. Disruption.

White working-class Americans used to be the rock that the American economy was built on, accounting in 1975 for 70 percent of the adult population. However, forty years later, that percentage had shrunk to 40 percent—the primacy of the white working-class man shriveling before our eyes.[11] Their anger, their hopelessness, is certainly understandable.

Why do we need disruptive thinking now? Ask that white rural man, who is staggered that his job prospects have disappeared, with no relief on the horizon. Ask that Black mother trying to figure out how to feed her family as her wages buy less with each passing month. Ask the worker gazing out the office window watching her CEO slide into the helicopter to ferry him to his private jet—as her health insurance coverage is slashed even further.

Trust has been shredded. Anger is the new American pastime. If we are to be saved, we desperately need to summon the power of disruptive thinking.

So, as we stand together on the precipice of the cliff, staring down into a valley teeming with unrelenting misery, we are all faced with the question for the ages: What are we going to do about it?

What disruption are we willing to make in our lives to bring about change?

For many of us, the misery index has been high for years. We have been immersed in despair for a long time, doing whatever we can to make it through another day and keep pushing forward—even when forward seems to offer nothing in the way of relief. But time spent in misery has no algebraic power over our ability to escape it. No matter how long it's been, we need to know that we don't have to stay there. I want to suggest to you that the new dream team for social justice comprises more than activists. It isn't merely going to be achieved through new presidents. The global village must unite with a resounding no. We must take our destiny from a one-pronged system of elected officials to galvanizing task forces that unite elected officials and CEOs focusing on diversity, equity, and inclusion not just because of a moral mandate but because it has proven to increase profitability.

We must make room at the table for spiritual leaders who have been tossed to the trash heap of the narrative, because we seem not to realize that their influence is priceless and that potential "wraparound" services accessorize social upward mobility. They possess the unique commodity of trust in many circles. Admittedly, we are becoming increasingly tribal. These social subsets all have their pastors, even if all of them aren't preachers. The legendary leadership of Bishop Charles Blake and his successor Presiding Bishop John Drew Sheard preside over the largest Pentecostal reformation of predominantly Black Pentecostals. We see the leadership of the current president of the National Baptist Convention of America, Dr. Samuel Tolbert, and the president of the Council of Bishops of the African Methodist Episcopal Church, Bishop Michael Leon Mitchell. Not to mention the tremendous "congregational" impact of forces like Charlamagne tha God, Oprah Winfrey, and Susan Taylor—although they are not pastors, they all have significant followings who listen to them closely. Many of them are contributors to transformative changes. Seth Godin, in his best-selling book *Tribes*, does a great job of reminding us that we all have spheres of influence. Not all of them are mammoth; influence isn't always relegated to the affluent or famous. It will take all of us—from Sean Combs to Jay-Z and Beyoncé, from former president Barack Obama and his highly respected wife, Michelle Obama, right down to John Doe and Sally Somebody. All are collarless clergy. All of them care, most are helping, but alliances are necessary to win. Now is the time for us all to join hands on the issues we can agree on. We will need to join hands across party lines, socioeconomic lines, racial lines, and gender divisions to agree on sustainable living. To unite around common causes on the critical issues is counterintuitive to the proclivity demonstrated among many today. People with PhDs must work shoulder to shoulder with people with GEDs to produce quantifiable impact and sustainable transformation, and to develop strategies that aren't merely limited to profit margins and election winners, uniting to form bridges of hope.

It's not one of us but all of us, myself included, who must step up and contribute by being change agents. I will talk more about how we are building bridges that we hope create additional change in housing, employment, and educational programs, all aimed at closing the canyons between us without replacing any of us. Recently the Dallas Regional Chamber appointed a task force to determine where our city ranked for diversity, equity, and inclusion (DEI). The results were shockingly dismal. In Dallas County, women earned 25 percent less than their male counterparts over a five-year time span from 2015 to 2020—lower than the national average of 18 percent less. While a majority of the 398 companies surveyed have DEI as a core value, less than half of those surveyed have any accountability in place to promote the values expressed. The Dallas region is 17 percent Black, yet only 5 percent of executives in the Dallas region were Black—Hispanics make up 31 percent of the region, and just 9 percent of executives are Hispanic. Tax incentives at the local, state, and federal levels could help corporations to be further incentivized for DEI. Spiritual leaders who see their responsibility beyond sermonizing must break our silence and develop solutions to a global crisis that is eating at the underbelly of the American dream. As clergy, we have a generation who will not hear our message if it isn't validated by some meaningful effort to close the pay gaps and increase the underrepresentation of marginalized groups—and work alongside the many CEOs and elected officials who want to close the pay gaps, the opportunity gaps, the digital divide, and the inevitable erosion of families. Economics remains the leading cause of divorce in this country—not infidelity, as I would've thought. Maybe instead of TV shows about cheaters, we should add a show about robbers—robbers of hope.

All of this creates opportunity. But only you, the recipient of said opportunities, can turn opportunities into reformative change.

Your moment has arrived—that final straw shoving you to the disruptive thought that can turn this thing around. Your now is here. You deserve fairness. You've earned peace. You merit fulfillment. The elements you need for your transformation, the disruptive steps you need to take, are already inside of you. They are sitting there, waiting. The only thing that can come out of you is what's already in you. Everything that Moses became he was. He was leading sheep around the desert, then he ended up leading people. David was a shepherd boy turned king, fending off lions and bears, and then Goliath, and then the Philistines, but he was always a warrior—a tender warrior.

Several years ago, my wife, Serita, decided she wanted to go back to school, at the tender age of sixty-one. She was maybe a semester and a half from finishing her college degree when she left school decades ago. When she told me her plans, my reaction could be summarized in one word: *Why?* We were exceedingly comfortable, had raised five successful children, and had seemingly everything we ever wanted. *Why did she need that?* But it was something she needed to prove to herself. She stayed up until four a.m. night after night doing homework. When she got her degree, we threw a big celebration party and had a good time. She took that step because she wanted to change.

I'm not here to set a goal for other people's lives—I'm here to show you how to attain the goal you set for your own life.

If you don't like the life you are living, you have the power to change it. It is inside of you. Fix it. Apologize. Say you're sorry. Do whatever it takes. If you don't like it, be complicit in the transformation you are praying for.

Recently I found myself screaming at the TV screen as they were interviewing a guy who was saying he couldn't get out of his neighborhood; he was trapped.

"That's not true!" I yelled.

If it is poverty keeping you there, you can be poor anywhere. You don't have to be poor and step over needles and bullets and guns. You can be poor in Texas, Mississippi, Western Virginia, or Arkansas and live in a cabin in the woods. You can be poor by the beach. It's not about money; it's about choices. Sometimes upward mobility begins with a change of environment. If you don't like your life, stop waiting for somebody to come change it. Change it yourself. Change. In the documentary *Waiting for Superman*, renowned educator Geoffrey Canada, founder of the Harlem Children's Zone, recounts how devastated he was as a child when he discovered that Superman—his favorite superhero—was a made-up character and would not be coming to save him and his family from the desolation of the South Bronx. So, Canada dedicated his life to uplifting children living in such conditions—in the process disrupting the educational orthodoxy's belief that "programs" and schools couldn't significantly move the needle for poor urban kids.

If you don't like your neighborhood, leave it. If you don't like your living room, paint it. I can't stress enough how strongly I feel about this. If you're miserable, change your life.

In our homes, in our families, people tolerate years and years of abuse and damage. They don't want to make any waves, and they don't want to make any noise, and they don't want to upset or disappoint anybody. Well, I say, *disappoint them*. Disappoint *all* of them. Find your way through the fog. Because you can't help anybody while you're bleeding yourself.

And let me be clear about something: this is not about money.

As our society increasingly values the pursuit and accumulation of riches, it has become ever clearer to me that in many ways this is a fool's errand. I don't mean to say that money can't bring untold pleasures to our lives, but it doesn't relieve the basic pain, strife, and struggle that are synonymous with the human experience.

You can accumulate all the riches in the world but still not feel like you matter. That is really what we all are seeking—to prove to ourselves that we matter. That may come from the satisfaction we get taking care of an old lady or a needy child. It can come from a vast variety of sources, from many different actions. In many ways, I'm still taking care of my father, a half century after he died. I do that by trying to take care of everybody around me, everybody in my purview. That's what drives me. How I tell myself I matter.

I have a friend whose brother was murdered in Washington, DC. Now my friend is raising his brother's son, and it's amazing to witness the person he has become. Because somebody needs him. He matters.

On the surface it may seem as if the pursuit of disruption and transformation would look different to someone in a poor marginal community as compared to someone in an upper-class community. After all, the wealthy person already has everything they need, right? Well, that's the case only if you believe that economy and money are the substrata of transformation. I'm here to tell you that they are not.

In early 2022, I spoke at a mega-conference of high-net-worth individuals created by a billionaire entrepreneur. Attendees had to pay upward of $30,000 to get into the conference—and it was sold out. To listen online cost $1,000. In my neck of the woods, that's pretty high cotton. The speaker who went before me was a former president. My host had asked me to speak on the topic of one of my books, *Don't Drop the Mic*, about the power of communication. I started out talking about the importance of communication in business and in relationships, but I moved into a much more personal realm for the attendees.

"You came here to learn how to make a lot of money, but what good is the money if you don't have peace?" I asked the crowd.

There is no difference between being suicidal in a ghetto and being suicidal in a mansion. The abundance of things we possess is not what gives us tranquility. So, when we start comparing poor communities, middle-class communities, and upper-class communities and wondering whether the wealthy folks actually need disruption and transformation, I say that none of us is exempt from having something we want to transform in our lives. The things we need may be different—although often they are not.

Everybody has some kind of poverty. Too many of us have been brainwashed to think if we have things, we don't have pain. That's not true at all. Sometimes you have more problems—more stress, more fear, more anxiety. Anorexia. Bulimia. Depression. Rich people have problems just like everybody else; they just live in a better house. When our society figures that out and stops being mad at them for being rich, we can connect on the bridge of human experience. Real wealth is affirmation, affection, humanity, and brotherhood. It's the look in your eye when you look at me and the look in my eye when I look at you. Those things transcend plans and barriers. Yes, poor people need to not be marginalized and to be transformed economically. But when they get there, to economic stability, they're going to find out that they still need to be transformed sociologically, psychologically, emotionally, or spiritually. And that can be just as hard and painful. None of us escapes this journey.

Disruption is necessary for the woman who's been beat over the head with a skillet, for the man whose wife is searching through his phone. Disruption becomes necessary to be free of all terrorists, foreign or domestic. You can have domestic terrorism not only in your country but in your house, on your job, in your life. And the fact that you make $1 million a month doesn't mean you're not terrorized.

When I broke that down to the wealthy crowd of influencers at the mega-conference, the whole place crumbled. I could see them collapse into tears. Because they knew that they were suffering—and they knew that I knew it. I don't have the money that they have, but I have enough money to know that money doesn't fix pain. We're all still human. You can't crawl into bed and cover yourself with your money to protect you. Money can't hold your hand when they're lowering your momma into the grave. When the doctor comes into the room to tell you your baby's dead, being rich doesn't make you feel any better. But we have glamorized success and wealth to the point where people are walking around thinking that those who have success and wealth don't have any problems. We're all human; we can't escape our skin. We're all clay. This is about your tenure and fitting in and being accepted—and not saying anything to get you tossed overboard.

You have many opportunities to disrupt your life to get the things you need, but your money isn't going to acquire them for you. Neither are fame and beauty. Some of the most confused people I've ever met were the most beautiful people—people so fine that I looked at them and wondered what it would be like to be that darn fine. Just-wake-up-in-the-morning fine. Ain't-brushed-your-teeth fine. Then I got to know them and found out they don't feel any different from the way I feel—and sometimes worse. I've had both men and women tell me that their looks are all that everyone sees. All of these experiences have let me know quite clearly that pain is not prejudiced; it attacks everybody.

So why do we need disruption now? Because we're all infected with different kinds of trauma. Herein lies the brother-hood of humanity. No tribe in the world has escaped it. We are desperately in need of something to be solved, inside or outside. The fierce urgency of now may not be an alarm from the outside. It may be an alarm from the inside. It may be an alarm in your marriage. It may be an alarm in your behavior. It may be an alarm in your addiction, or your drinking, or your neuroses, or your gambling. It may be something that you're sick of. That's your urgency. It's not always about changing the world. It starts with changing your world. And then hopefully, one change at a time, we can change our world. But it doesn't happen until you get a grip on your world—because isn't that all that really matters to you at the end of the day? Before we grab the lofty notions of changing the political system and the housing system and the banking system, let's change the atmosphere in the house.

Let's take more baths in soothing water and play soft music and light candles. Perhaps your peace comes from a meditative moment on the back porch and a transformative hour of listening to the crickets as the sun sets. Let's be peace-ridden with appreciation, so that when we do get ready to be innovative, we have something to spend. Because the bankruptcy of the soul is when more is going out than what's coming in. We have to be very intentional about keeping our emotional checkbook balanced. It's easy to write more checks than we get deposits. Disruptive thinking means we have to be purposeful about allowing people into our life that feed us, not just need us. We can't keep feeding if we can't keep eating; we're going to go bankrupt. Disruptive thinking shatters the norm of what we need. That's why it's so personal. My wife may not be what you need; your wife may not be what I need. You may need more space; I may need less. This is a tailored design.

Success to me is when what I envisioned in my head appears in front of my eyes. The outer working of the internal—when the joy of my life starts with a concept in my head and I watch it incubate and develop in front of my eyes until it mirrors what I saw in my head. Whether it's a message or a movement or a business deal or a community build or getting one of my kids to be what I thought they could be. Disruptive thinking for each of us is personal, specific, individually transformative.

Let's take that disruptive thought. Now.

THREE

DISRUPTIVE PARTNERSHIPS

When I was a teenager playing the piano for a community group, a young man who lived in my neighborhood and sang in my group was arrested. This didn't happen in our community every day, so it was shocking. I knew him well, so it was also painful to observe. How could this happen to someone I grew up next to? Our parents were friends. I walked past his house every day. Over fifty years later, I still pastor some of his family members. He was arrested and indicted primarily because he happened to be in the wrong car at the wrong time and ended up getting sentenced on an armed robbery charge. Even though he had no guns, he was with people who did, and now he had to pay the price. And even though he was a minor, he was tried as an adult and sent away to a maximum-security facility. This kid was no more criminal than I am an astronaut.

But what can you do when your resources are limited, your influence is inconsequential, and you fit the stereotypical image of news reports? You look like what is often portrayed as an objectification of all that's wrong in the world. Your options are minimal, so strip-searched and legs gapped, you are introduced to an alternate reality. You will likely lose your chance at education, your right to ever vote. Trauma untreated is your only company.

And much of this is the systemic hustle of backroom plea bargaining deals, indifferent court-appointed attorneys with heavy caseloads and little pay, auctioned and traded for a strong statistic to become a district attorney's talking point in a campaign speech for the next midterm election. Hands cuffed, mother weeping, heart racing, and off you go . . . locked up with dangerous people who will do God knows what to a frightened little Black boy who sang in my choir.

Our choir decided to visit the prison and do a concert. We drove several hours in a cavalcade of cars of hope to encourage his heart and show we cared. However, love didn't diminish my sweating palms, my speeding pulse, and my sudden awareness that this concert could be dangerous on a whole lot of levels. I will never forget the feeling of being processed in that prison and having the steel doors slammed behind me. The bolted door sealed me from a freedom I was accustomed to. But soon it would open my eyes to the first course of America's "tough on crime" policies. It gave me an up-close view that resulted in an increased awareness that every man and woman in the prisons was more than the number they were called in the database—they were all someone's child, and many had lost their way. Seventy percent of them were incarcerated on nonviolent crimes, as American politicians had popularized a "tough on crime" campaign rhetoric. And yes, it got votes, but it also ripped apart families, did psychological damage, and tore at the soul of our disproportionately Black and brown youth placed in criminal environments. And though they were no worse than the opioid drug dealers of the good old boys, the minority population couldn't afford the representation that wins trials.

So we did what all our ancestors did when they felt helpless: we sang, we prayed, and before we left, we cried. The steel doors closed, but my eyes flew open—and they're still open today. And just in case yours might not be open, allow me an opportunity to sound an alarm that helps you to see that what I'm thinking may penetrate the dysfunctionality without dismissing the dire need to remain vigilant against crime.

The United States is the most prolific jailer in the world. A staggering 20 percent of the total prison population on the planet currently sits in US penal institutions—more than 2 million people.[1] The US makes up only 4 percent of the global population. Clearly, we have made significant investments in the idea that we can jail our way out of societal problems like crime. Except it doesn't work. Numerous studies have shown that increasing incarceration rates don't lower crime. But they do have a devastating impact on individuals, families, and communities, wrecking everyone in their ravenous path.

Because our society makes it so difficult for convicted people to successfully reenter society after they serve their time—gainful employment is difficult if not impossible to find, housing resources are limited, and even accessing student aid is nearly hopeless—nearly half of them eventually return to prison. The costs to our society, not to mention our families and communities, are staggering.

I knew I had to do something to turn this around. We had to find a way to provide stability and security for these returning individuals so they could access the kind of gainful employment and housing that would restore their pride and sense of purpose. We needed to disrupt the prison industrial complex and shut off the pipeline of humanity keeping it in business. In 2005, I founded the Texas Offenders Reentry Initiative (TORI) to fight back against this system. I'm extremely proud of the work we've done. Over the years, we've served over thirty thousand returning citizens—and our recidivism rate is 11 percent, just a fraction of the national average.

In the paragraph above, there is one word that should stand out: *we*. There is no way I could have done this alone. Crucially, TORI needed to form partnerships with employers who would give these individuals a job—a chance to rebuild their lives. One of the most meaningful partnerships I formed was with Randall Stephenson, the former CEO of AT&T. When I first sat down to talk with Stephenson, who was still head of AT&T at the time, on the surface we couldn't have been more different. He was running a massive organization with more than two hundred thousand employees. I had about three hundred employees. He's white; I'm Black. Yet we partnered together because we found something that united us, something that we galvanized around—finding a path for ex-offenders to have job opportunities that would disrupt recidivism. Quickly, we discovered there was more to unite us than there was to divide us. And though we only got to the early stages of our program before he retired, it started a wave that still continues.

Meaningful partnerships are often unlikely alliances. Nowhere is this more explicit than the story of the Good Samaritan, which I referred to in chapter 1. This story comes after Jesus says the greatest commandments are to love God with all your heart, mind, and soul, and to love your neighbor as yourself. A young lawyer tries to trap him by asking a very granular question: "Who is my neighbor?" In response, Jesus tells the story of the Samaritan who helped the bleeding man on the road to Jericho. The hemorrhaging of our communities is much like the bleeding of the man on the road. His rescuer wasn't the Levite or the priest, but the unlikely Samaritan. To find a solution from our troubles may require all of us to stop working in silos and find common ground for substantive change.

There is nothing worse than being disruptive and being alone. Not only is it emotionally challenging, but we are likely to be less effective. We are most productive when we have a whole community of people who galvanize around that disruption and support it. In order for reentry programs like TORI to work, we have to find places that will employ the ex-offenders. This means partnering with companies willing to engage in some disruptive thinking themselves by stepping away from the conventional view that it is somehow dangerous to hire someone who has been incarcerated. The conventional view throws people away. It is disruptive to embrace them and give them an opportunity to prove that they matter.

Just because you're a disruptive thinker, that doesn't mean you have all the components to complete the assignment. Developing partnerships requires that we recognize our limitations. We have to be disruptive enough to put ego to the side, which will enable us to find partners who bring substance to the table that can accessorize our limitations. Partnering with somebody who's good at what we're not allows us to accomplish the things we see. Taking these steps will require humility and introspection. We have to identify the areas where we need help, where our skills or resources won't get the job done.

For too many of us, when we think about forming partnerships, we turn to what we know and like—people who went to the same school we did, grew up in our neighborhood, or go to the same church. But to move forward, we often have to open our mind to the idea that God may use somebody who doesn't connect with us on everything but connects with us on this thing.

Civil rights leaders in the 1950s who were pushing for the federal government to finally pass laws that would strike down legal segregation and recognize the humanity of all Americans saw Texas senator Lyndon B. Johnson as a resolute member of the opposition. After all, this was a man whose racism was so intense that when he was discussing a piece of civil rights legislation with other Southern lawmakers in the 1950s, he referred to it as the "nigger bill," according to Johnson biographer Robert Caro.

But after the assassination of John F. Kennedy, civil rights leaders formed a profoundly unlikely alliance with the newly installed President Johnson. Johnson used threats, bribes, and even physical intimidation to help push through the Civil Rights Act of 1964, which crushed Jim Crow, and the Voting Rights Act of 1965, which prohibited racial discrimination in voting. In addition, Johnson's "War on Poverty" set the government on a more progressive path to improving the living conditions of poor Americans.

But these monumental actions shouldn't be taken as a signal that Johnson had fundamentally changed. After Johnson nominated the already well-known Thurgood Marshall to the Supreme Court in 1967, he reportedly explained his decision, according to biographer Robert Dallek, by saying, "when I appoint a nigger to the bench, I want everybody to know he's a nigger."

History provides another potent example of the power of unlikely alliances with the 1955 Montgomery bus boycott. After Rosa Parks was arrested for refusing to give up her seat on a city bus, leaders in the Black community called for a boycott of Montgomery's public buses to demonstrate their unified protest of segregated seating. But that led to enormous logistical problems, as they would have to provide somewhere around twenty thousand rides per day to Black laborers who had to get to work. Having a car was out of the financial reach of many Black families in 1955; car owners were among the wealthiest Black people in town. Martin Luther King Jr. and other leaders had to call on these wealthy folks to lend their vehicles to the boycott effort. King was shocked when more than 150 car owners signed up to hand over their cars at a public meeting in December at the start of the boycott.

"The automobile was still among the prime status symbols in the United States, and therefore to volunteer one's car as public transportation was a radical act of togetherness," Taylor Branch wrote in *Parting the Waters: America in the King Years, 1954–63*. "The fractious classes of Montgomery's Negroes now promised to blend their daily lives."

The boycott was sustained for an astounding thirteen months, one of the most impressive displays of Black alliances in American history. It ended with the Supreme Court ruling that segregation on public buses is unconstitutional.

In the Bible, Cyrus the Great is mentioned more than thirty times—even though Cyrus is a Persian who doesn't even believe in Jehovah. This pagan king is important in Jewish history because it was under his rule that Jews were first allowed to return to Israel after seventy years in captivity.

In one of the most amazing prophecies of the Bible, the Lord revealed Cyrus's decree to free the Jews to Isaiah. One hundred fifty years before Cyrus lived, the prophet calls Cyrus by name and gives details of Cyrus's benevolence to the Jews: "This is what the Lord says to his anointed, to Cyrus, whose right hand I take hold of to subdue nations before him . . . 'I summon you by name and bestow on you a title of honor, though you do not acknowledge me'" (Isa. 45:1 NIV, 4; see also 41:2–25; 42:6). Evincing His sovereignty over all nations, God says of Cyrus, "He is my shepherd and will accomplish all that I please" (Isa. 44:28 NIV).

This is a thoroughly unlikely alliance. Cyrus was a pagan king, yet God calls him anointed and "His shepherd." God partners with an unbeliever to deliver His people, even anointing him for the task.

At its most granular level, marriage is an unlikely alliance. Two people with different backgrounds, different histories, and different ways of looking at the world come together with the expectation that they will be able to coexist. People often tell them to communicate, not understanding that what is meant by words like *trust, love, support, family, unity,* and *normalcy* have different interpretations based on different people's experiences and family dynamics. In order for a marriage to be successful, there must be a degree of dismantling of past family cultures and experiences. They must be refitted to a new family construct that takes place in a different era, often in a different location, and amid changing economic, emotional, and sexual realities. How disruptive is that? In order to pull this off, we need enormous patience, understanding, empathy, and sensitivity. But I think we often dive into marriage without considering the work the partnership will require. This naïveté is likely a huge reason why the national divorce rate is so high—about 50 percent of married couples in the US eventually divorce.

My own marriage is a prime example of unlikely alliances. My wife and I are two very different people. I'm an extrovert, while Serita is an introvert. What energizes me exhausts her; what energizes her can drive me up the wall. While I'm writing, I may have the music playing and the TV going. It doesn't bother me to have all this stimulation flying at me at once. My wife is quite different. She likes quiet, tranquility. Her workspace feels more like a spa—candles burning, soft music playing, if there's any music at all. It's what she needs. One of our biggest early mishaps was giving each other what *we* need rather than understanding the other person and what they need.

We had to learn how to live together, how to have these two distinct worlds coexist. What makes this even more challenging is one of the peculiarities of human nature: the differences that attract in the beginning often later repel. Most marriages end up on a course of self-justification to determine who is right, rather than acknowledging their differences. In order to achieve compromise, both will have to be willing to disrupt to some degree their assumptions about what is normal to create what will be a new normal, mutually agreed-upon core values, and a path to realignment that respects what was but is also willing to sacrifice the familiar for the health of the future.

The same realities are also true when we partner with organizations, consultants, and people outside of our normal business orbit. We have to go through the same process of learning about one another and developing mutual respect. That means not falling into the trap of thinking the other person is wrong and needs to be retrofitted into our culture. Instead, you might need to realize that new people are beneficial only if you are willing to consider new methods that might provide improved results.

When Serita and I go on vacation, we have very different ideas of what fun looks like. We're both excited as we pack and envision being together in some lovely place. I'm excited because I'm going to get away from all the work and the bustling activity that's always swirling around me. I get to be a guy and she gets to be a girl, and we're gonna have a great time spicing up the romance and seeing the sights. If it's the beach, I've envisioned nice swimwear, cute negligees, evening wear for dinners, hiking boots for trails, romantic music for luxurious moments in bubbling Jacuzzis, right? Nooo, that's not what she is envisioning, though we both are excited about getting away. What she's thinking is, *I don't have to put on any makeup. I don't have to worry about getting the kids out the door. I get to lie in bed and sleep.* That's an ideal vacation to her. It's clear we're going into this with two different versions of ideal. So I had to learn. It's not that she won't go out to see the sights—just don't expect her to go in the morning. I might go out and scout all the places I want to go and the things I want to see. Then I come back to the hotel. She has had a chance to sleep in, to chill. Come the afternoon, she's ready to join me on new adventures—and I'm rescued from bouncing off the walls in the hotel room, fuming. That's how we've managed to stay married for forty years—negotiating beyond differences and finding commonalities by working toward solutions.

Disruptive thinking has to climb over the hurdles of unlikely alliances, initial discomfort, and possible misunderstandings, and find solutions that work. Just because you make the acquisition doesn't mean you are ready for the operations. In business, one must consider more than liquid assets and buy out options from a contractual perspective. The adaptability of the company is just as critical as the adaptability of a companion. An atmosphere of mutual respect is an absolute prerequisite for a new entity to emerge, void of old baggage from past experiences. Bring a large wrecking ball to old norms and listen for the crumbling of what may have nostalgic significance. It can only happen when both entities have a great allegiance to what's possible and a willingness to disrupt what was to get there.

The differences may actually work to our benefit, giving us the opportunity to see matters from a completely new angle, a new perspective—one that may never have occurred to us if we continue to work in silos. It is possible to do good in business, in marriage, and in life without compromising doing well. We cannot benefit from alliances if we aren't willing to be altered by them. Change is imminent.

The parent-child relationship is another example of a vital alliance that often can mean bringing together two entities that aren't a natural fit. But if those two parties don't figure out how to make it work, problems can rush in like a flood. Most parents have made the discovery that the child who is easiest to parent is the one whose personality profile is most like our own. You just "get" them. You understand what bothers them and what sets their heart racing. When something goes down, you understand why they're mad, because you would have been mad if that had happened to you. You know exactly how your brooding introvert will react when Grandma is prying for more information about her new boyfriend—because you used to react the exact same way to the same questions. When the child has gone silent, you know precisely what the silence means.

But that other kid, the gregarious social butterfly? You haven't a clue. Their personality is foreign to you. Sometimes that child gets less attention from you. Or you have fewer meaningful conversations with that child. You're not even sure why. You ask your spouse, "Why won't she talk to me? How come every time she wants something, she goes to you—even though I was sitting right there?"

Your spouse has to give you a debriefing, to explain the child to you. The alliance is unbreakable—the kid is always going to be yours—but that doesn't mean it's going to be effective. The effectiveness of the alliance depends on your ability to observe the other, understand them, appreciate them, and learn how to communicate with them. *Observation* is key. It doesn't always come naturally, but it is critical. It must be combined with *communication*. Communication without observation can lead to some wrong-headed conclusions, as does observation without communication. You might notice something, but you still have to discuss it to really understand what it means.

When my wife and I were going on a recent vacation, we were both excited. As I said, what she envisioned as an exciting vacation was very different from what I envisioned. We had two different goals. To get past that, we continue to ask each other a critical question: "What do you need from me *now*?" That's how we've stayed together for forty years. Because people change. And most marriages fail because the person is busy giving you what you used to need. People don't come with updates like computers and cellphones. The same is true of any partnership—you have to keep checking in, updating your operating system.

As a parent, you have to be secure enough to accept differences. Your child is not you. There's no reason why you should expect that child to have the same personality as you, like the same meals and activities you like, and communicate in the same way as you do. And you have to be okay with that. Your job is to give them attention and affirmation, even though you're a football player and your son is a pianist. You had dreams of watching him racing across the field catching touchdown passes. But when you throw him the ball, he embarrasses you in front of your friends because he can't catch worth a darn. But he can play the hell out of Mozart. The partnership can still work, as long as you do your part—observe and communicate. This is true in every area of our lives.

The manager-employee relationship, which is one that looms over so many of our lives in good and bad ways, can often be an unlikely alliance. These relationships frequently begin when an employee is promoted to manager and now must undergo a reorientation of how they think. They must go from being me-centered to we-centered; their locus of concern suddenly must extend far wider than it did before. The employee probably thought about the company's bottom line in a distant, abstract way—similar to how they thought about the national debt or the backlog in the state's court system. Important stuff, sure, but not something that's going to keep them tossing and turning at night. As a manager, however, they could very well affect the company's quarterly profits with a couple of dumb decisions. How they perform matters to a lot more people.

Newly promoted managers are in trouble if they continue to think like employees. Yes, they can be better managers if they retain the ability to see matters from the employee perspective. But now they have to care about budgets and bills, ledgers and licenses, key performance indicators and those annoying memos from the back office informing them of company policy changes, new IRS regulations and health department guidelines, human resources policy updates and so much more. Their perspective has to broaden. If they fail to make that transition, they're not going to survive. Just because someone gets promoted doesn't mean they automatically have the tools to do the new job. They need to do some homework to understand their new role. They have to fellowship with a different circle of people to understand the mentality—because it's not just learning facts; it's learning a different way of looking at your environment and redefining the metrics of success. Now you know how much toilet paper it takes for your hotel to operate, and the size of the water bill from washing all the towels the guests didn't even use. Now you're thinking about the wear and tear on the hotel rugs—whereas before you couldn't care less about those rugs you walked over every day.

In my household, December can be an aggravating time of year for me. I'm thinking about property taxes, quarterly taxes, end-of-year statements, collecting receipts, FICA, insurance renewals—all the things I need to pay. In addition, I have to transform into Santa Claus and pay for everybody's Christmas and make sure we've got enough turkey on the table. That is not Serita's perspective. I'm worried about things she is not considering. She's thinking about the decorations that got broken over the year and the platter for the roasted turkey that somebody dropped. I need to be sympathetic to what's important to her while understanding that she's not thinking about any of the things I'm thinking about. It's not a matter of whose worries are more important; they're just different. The alliance of these two perspectives has to work in order for the end result to be what we both want. We have different responsibilities, different roles. Now that she has her own company, her list is growing and is much more diverse than when the children were small. However, for any partnership to work, there has to be reciprocity. What each partner brings has to be different—not competitive but complementing our unique nuances. Otherwise, why are we partnering in the first place?

When we are thrust into new partnerships, one of the most critical responses is *observation*. We must be extremely observant, attuned to our surroundings, open to the possibility that we don't understand what we're doing or seeing. None of us steps into a new situation with all the knowledge we will need to thrive. We're going to have to figure some stuff out. One of the best ways of doing that is to observe everything. Assume nothing.

There are likely going to be both spoken and unspoken rules, things you can't pick up from textbooks or manuals or classrooms. School isn't going to be enough to save you. Because everything that's true in corporate America, or in a marriage, is not in the textbook. You can have a doctorate of divinity, but that doesn't mean you can pastor people. You can know the Apocrypha, be able to dissect the Nicene Creed, and be an expert on church history, but when you walk into that pulpit you are dealing directly with people whose mother just died in their arms, or whose baby wasn't breathing when it emerged from the birth canal. None of that theology they taught you prepares you to deal with a deacon who is gambling away his paycheck. There are no classes to prepare you for the situations that will be thrust upon you. You must go from comforting a wailing family at a funeral to a meeting with the bank about getting the parking lot paved. You have to be extremely flexible to do that. You have to be adept at handling problems—and then walk out into the pulpit on Sunday morning like there are no problems. Because people don't come to church to hear about the problems that are bubbling up at the church. The roof is leaking, somebody slipped on the ice and is suing us—you don't want to hear me preach about that.

Leadership isn't easy, and alliances are even less so. Disruption can be frightening. Yet without it, we would still be riding wagons to country general stores to get supplies and horse feed. It generally takes some adverse winds to break the concrete of normal and dig out the path to what previously would've been impossible. In many ways, the tragic and senseless death of George Floyd has been the impetus of new discussions and odd alliances, as most Americans began to realize that everyone who lives in your city isn't having the same experiences. Add that to the disproportionate deaths of Black and brown people to COVID-19 and the result was government officials, scientists, clergy, and corporations started talking across the fence and looking at the possibility that maybe we do need each other to bring systemic change in a lasting and meaningful way.

In a partnership, it's vital to understand what's important to your strategic partners and a broader alliance of constituents if winning is to be attained. That understanding doesn't just come from boardroom meetings. It might be something you learn on the golf course, over dinner, or on a coffee break. There are many different ways of getting to know your new partners and what concerns them. But what has become increasingly clear with every shooting, report of police brutality, or variant of novel coronavirus is that we must pay the most earnest heed to finding a way to have a conversation and work with the resulting outcomes without controlling the narratives and succumbing to our propensity for pure narcissistic gain.

The great news is that new pathways are beginning to emerge in our collective human community as we come together to build the underserved areas that should have never been neglected in the first place. And corporations are starting to consider their sociological responsibility to solve problems both within and without their spheres of direct oversight by engagement beyond traditional alliances and fiduciary responsibility to shareholders.

In Dallas, we worked with students and their brilliant teachers in building a new and exciting curriculum around marketing, coding, and production, leading to a packed theater for them to see the live performance of *Hamilton*, the renowned play written by Lin-Manuel Miranda. It was only made possible because of a partnership between the Moody Foundation, Atmos Energy, the Meadows Foundation, the T.D. Jakes Foundation, and Frito-Lay. Later we repeated the same process with these organizations to expose the children to the hit production *Ain't Too Proud to Beg,* both held at Broadway Dallas. We provided resources to struggling school systems to close the digital divide and increase an appreciation for the arts, technology, production, and marketing. We saw a tremendous impact in a multiple-week training course that culminated in attending the amazing theatrical productions. It was an unlikely alliance, but it worked.

Many years ago, I attended a small but profound gathering of high-octane ministers and scholars called Conversations, hosted by Dr. Walter Thomas, the senior pastor of New Psalmist Baptist Church in Baltimore. It was there that I had the privilege of listening at the unique and impactful presentation of the Right Reverend Floyd Flake, the prominent African Methodist Episcopal pastor and a former congressman. Rev. Flake had unique insights due to his duality of experiences within government and as a strong advocate for community development. He shared a very disruptive idea while addressing us about speaking truth to power. He said that you think you're speaking truth to power when you speak to elected officials, but there is another layer of power beneath that power. We were shocked when he identified that the hidden power of incredible influence was Exxon, Mobil Oil, McDonald's, and other such corporations of the world, which he said were not to be underestimated in their ability to impact policy and influence culture. He was telling us that these corporations have incredible influence with elected officials. At the time, few people realized that unions, teachers' unions, the NRA, and major corporations have an unrivaled ability to influence outcomes—a fact that has since become more visible to the general public.

Today, corporations are starting to step up in other even more significant ways. Contemporary CEOs have used that power beyond affecting their bottom lines by engaging in creating a more equitable society, making the necessary changes to expand workforce hiring, job readiness, educational pathways, and financial literacy. Perhaps it's because of a newfound moral sensibility as a new generation of leaders take the helm, or maybe because they recognize that their own sustainability demands a broader-based clientele.

Some who had been AWOL, whose silence had been deafening, are waking to the realization that we are a collective aggregation of humanity. There cannot be alignment without agreement. Wells Fargo, Bank of America, JPMorgan Chase, Walmart, and Chick-fil-A are starting to gather around the table to solve inequities or at least diminish them. This is indeed an exciting turn of events as the ideas of diversity, equity, and inclusion (DEI) have begun infiltrating the ethos of major corporations. Additionally, environment, social impact, and governance (ESG) ratings have become more significant in how corporations do business. Yes, there are legitimate reasons for the reluctance; risk management and brand alignment were concerns in the past and still are today. But there is also the potential to find common ground. We have seen an increase in accountability—not only in responsibility to shareholders but also governance compliance. And social media has given every person the power to become a whistleblower. Community engagement has disrupted the myopic scope of profit and now includes a newfound sense of shared responsibility to all citizens.

Many times the propensity to do business with people you know both intentionally and occasionally unintentionally avoids people you do not. We are in the process of shattering the traditional good old boys' clubs; women, members of the LGBTQ community, and minorities are now being invited to have a seat at the table. Like it or not, we are watching a huge disruption in the "good old days"—which weren't so good for everyone. No matter which of these factors are the overwhelming impetuses for change, it's starting to happen. But much like getting hit by a bus, intentions don't resuscitate the victim.

The wisdom of Jesus shows segments of diversity in the selection of His disciples. Though He originally didn't make an obvious clarion call for women on his board of disciples, his choice of disciples is extremely diverse. His inner circle of twelve disciples wasn't composed of twelve rabbis, but dreaded tax collectors, blue-collar workers, business leaders, and physicians. And the truth is that some of his strongest supporters economically and most loyal supporters physically were women, like Joanna (see Luke 12: 3).

Our leadership should be reflective of our society. Traditionally, corporations, unlike politicians, have shied away from engaging religion of any kind and certainly not Black churches. Distribution channels have been barricaded for most Black business products except the endorsement deals of athletes. Most important, extending capital to help Black business scale up hasn't been treated as a viable option. But we are now seeing instances where disruptive thinking is proposing a path forward that reflects better ESG conscientiousness. This is vital news, especially since faith still significantly impacts Black culture, according to Barna Group research and my own eyes. In terms of gender, Black women have often turned elections around and, unfortunately, represent the majority of heads of households in our community; they are now being heard and seen. We are watching the trends closely.

Charlie Scharf, Wells Fargo's new CEO who was a protégé of JPMorgan Chase CEO Jamie Dimon, was brought in almost like an executive gunslinger to clean up many of the less savory and sometimes unscrupulous practices of Wells Fargo that adversely affected minorities that were well documented under previous regimes. Although there is still a lot of work to be done, he is certainly a person of interest in the transformation of Wells Fargo. Doug McMillon, the CEO of Walmart, whom I first met in New Orleans at the Essence Music Festival, seems to be moving toward community engagement and enhanced employment opportunities in fresh ways.

Can they achieve their goal? Only time will tell, but what I do know is that there are interesting steps being taken toward correction—steps that are sorely needed. Many of these companies are willing to take the road less traveled and leave the comfort zone of the norms of the old guard by aligning with the Urban League, working with the NAACP, employing independent social justice auditors, supporting the National Association of Black Journalists, and working with real estate developers in strategic alliances to tackle some of the socioeconomic conundrums of our previously ignored community and those of others.

We aren't there yet, but every step moves us from the brink of losing our middle class and increasing the impoverished to getting closer to Dr. King's long overdue dream. The share of American adults who live in households considered to be middle class fell from 61 percent in 1971 to 50 percent in 2021, according to a Pew Research Center analysis of government data.[2] Not disappeared, but certainly imperiled. I'm hoping like-minded people stand together for all people neglected or marginalized in our society to form pathways for the betterment of all. I often say that I've seldom seen anyone mugged by someone who had to go to work in the morning! Here in America and around the world, COVID-19, racism, predatory lending, and the lack of new skill sets needed to remain competitive may have made it more difficult, but still it is not impossible. That's my dream, my legacy—and hopefully yours. If all of us do something, we can accomplish anything without losing what we've worked hard to build. This isn't a plea for a replacement theory but a relationship-building opportunity.

We don't have to conform on every issue to participate in the transformation if we can find points of alignment. This is not only a nonpartisan issue, but also a "we the people" prerequisite. Whether in business, marriage, life, or ministry, there have to be strategic alignments. Our endeavors to uplift underserved communities in significant and tangible ways, put technology in the reach of our children, close food deserts, bring mixed-income housing opportunities to underserved communities, increase green spaces, expand job opportunities, improve workforce readiness, and make sure science, technology, engineering, arts, and math education is brought to the forefront (as jobs in those sectors are rapidly increasing and do not have enough women or minority participation) will require partnerships. We are the people we have been waiting on!

Yes, I'm attempting to be a voice, not in the streets but in the boardrooms where decisions are made. Historically, we have drawn attention to oppression on a street level. That's very important. But transformation also happens in boardrooms, not just through protest and bullhorns. We need both, but too often, what is screamed in the bullhorn isn't repeated in the boardroom. It's hard to get in the boardroom. Houston, we have contact!

But these new alliances are new territory and new partnerships, and the possibilities spark hope. It was important from the onset of our relationship with entities like Wells Fargo to ascertain expectations and see if their intentions were to disrupt the past to correct the future. I'm left pondering what *better* would look like. For the investment of influence, effort, and capital, how do we quantify our goals? I want to know how we are being measured. Is it how many people we touch? Is it how many people we give grants to? Is it how many people we help with deposits to get in houses? What are the metrics on social impact? It was necessary to carve out what the expectation is, so we can know what success looks like for both parties in order to win. Alliances are, or should be, built on alignment.

Oftentimes when we're coming together with unlikely partners, we get caught up in the differences between us. It's tempting to throw up our hands when we encounter differences. When in fact, it is often the uniquenesses that increase the impact. We need to be focused on solutions. Not every merger works, no more than every marriage does. There has to be some connective tissue for a graph to take place. Often a gradual approach is better than a quick plunge. Not every succession plan works. It is sometimes difficult to identify which "odd couples" have the nimbleness and adaptability to survive what some others do not.

I always laugh when elderly couples are interviewed. They're often asked what the secret of a long-lasting relationship is. The often-varied answers leave puzzled students. I'm not sure we can have absolute certainty amid honking horns and tossed rice which couples' nuptials will last and which couples will not. Longevity isn't just a science; it's an art. Adaptability quotients within the organization, marriage, ministry, or company are critical for withstanding downturns, inflation, empty nests, or menopause.

It is time for you to do your assessment of the unions you make in your profession or your home. The question isn't just "Are they a good fit for where I am?" The better question is "Can they exhibit nimbleness necessary to evolve as needs change and circumstances are altered?" Inflexibility can turn disruption into destruction. Being too inflexible is detrimental to growth. We must often function in an ever-evolving environment without losing our core values.

When AT&T moved to acquire Time Warner in 2016, AT&T CEO Randall Stephenson called the pair "a perfect match," stressing their "complementary strengths." However, it was certainly an unlikely alliance—a phone company stepping into the movie business. They struggled to figure out how to work together; making movies is an entirely different mindset than making phones. They had to figure out how to take these two distinct worlds and merge them into a seamless whole. Three years after the deal went through, AT&T had

had enough—the company unwound its $85 billion purchase of Time Warner and merged its media properties with Discovery. The alliance apparently wasn't as seamless as the parties had hoped.

In successful partnerships, role models are vital. Space programs start with models; builders start with drawings; films start with scripts. Modeling affects every part of our society. If there is no model, there is no chance to adapt and reconstruct. Mentoring is great, but I see young men and women every day trying to be what was not modeled in front of them. To be honest, it was difficult to find my way to manhood in the absence of a viable model. I graphically and personally know what happens when there is no model. Often we have to seek out models rather than imagine that we can reach our destination when life provides no GPS, map, or model to guide us to what's next.

When many older African Americans were growing up, particularly in the years before integration, we were exposed to the spectrum of the Black experience. We saw how doctors and lawyers and engineers lived because they owned the house next door or down the street. We were able to witness marriages that thrived and those that faltered—and to see the differences in how the partners operated in the marriage. But as integration allowed Black professionals to move into predominantly white neighborhoods, the nature of Black neighborhoods changed. Middle-class families fled, creating communities where most households were mired in acute poverty. The role models were gone. Though it's often well intentioned, building low-income housing as opposed to creating mixed-income housing resulted in disasters, loss of community pride, and loss of access to models for sustainable change.

One study showed that if children of low-income parents grow up in counties where they can make friends with children from high-income families, their incomes in adulthood increase by an average of 20 percent. Researchers like Harvard economist Raj Chetty have chronicled the devastating effect that living in overwhelmingly poor neighborhoods can have on the ability of children to rise out of poverty.[3]

When poor Black boys live in neighborhoods where many children have fathers in the home, research shows that they fare better—even if their own fathers weren't present. Having men in their midst provided them with role models and mentors who could guide them toward more positive activities. I've seen this happen up close, over and over, throughout my life.

Black children who move to areas with low poverty rates, low racial bias, and higher father presence earlier in their childhood have higher incomes and lower rates of incarceration as adults. But the challenge is that very few Black children grow up in such surroundings. That puts the onus on us—we have to do a better job of building such neighborhoods.

One of the newer companies I created is T.D. Jakes Real Estate Ventures. A primary focus of the company is building mixed-use, mixed-income housing, where families from different income levels will live together and learn from each other. That's a classic case of unlikely alliances. Residents need to see somebody in the neighborhood doing better than they are. Young children can see before their eyes, within their reach, the existence of role models. Children are now going to school with kids who take school seriously. They start seeing ways to elevate themselves that don't involve rhyming in a microphone or dribbling a basketball. They see adults running to Walmart, helping their kids with homework, sitting on the back porch reading a book—instead of smoking a blunt.

I think one of the reasons Black women are doing so well is because of abundant role models. Black girls don't have to look far to see impressive examples to emulate—from Michelle Obama and Kamala Harris in politics, to Maya Angelou and Cicely Tyson in the arts, to Sarah Vaughan and Jill Scott in music, to Oprah Winfrey, Venus Williams, and Serena Williams in business. The list is endless, from Harriet Tubman to Fannie Lou Hamer and Rosa Parks. These are our mothers and sisters, daughters and aunts. They've had as tough a time as their counterparts like Jackie Robinson, Paul Robeson, John Lewis, Martin Luther King Jr., Sidney Poitier, and Denzel Washington. The difference, however, is these women had to deal with the intersectionality of being Black and a woman. In my day and my neighborhood, the teachers were heroes. The dentists and doctors were held in high esteem. Even the preachers were a lot more revered than now. Women had an especially hard road both publicly and privately. Often one's success came at the expense of the other.

Phrases like *Black girls rock* and *Black girl magic* aren't an attempt to discriminate against white women or even Black men. They're an attempt to self-heal sociological and historical inequities that have festered and been ignored by people who have not endured the trauma associated with their experiences. Yes, liver cancer is lethal and can be deadly, but chronic breast cancer organized tremendous public attention as it ravished women of all colors. Yet, we don't picket and say "All cancer matters." That's obvious! A whole lot of successful women had to disrupt the good old boys' club to get a seat at the table that is still tenuous at best. Black men, and perhaps men in general, are trying to find that ability to dismantle vicious social constructs that seem to not shine a light on a path forward or even a model to disrupt the prison pipeline. They're struggling to achieve opportunities while more jobs are going to technology and artificial intelligence. Yes, we can boast a great deal of accomplishments, but if we don't find a way to turn around neighborhoods and build up families, refocus our faith institutions and strengthen our HBCUs, the consequences will be devastating for the nation.

The statistics already are staggering, especially for our boys. The entirety of the income gap between Black and white people is due to the deprivation of Black males—Black women are keeping pace with white people. We lost a community of role models within our reach, and the bill we are paying is the annihilation of many Black men who lacked the skills and resources to move forward in a strategic sequence of transformative ideas. The likely erosion of affirmative action will elevate even higher the role of HBCUs, as they already deliver around 70 percent of degreed Black people. In the third decade of the twenty-first century, we are looking at a generation of children who will become adults less well-off than their parents. The concept of generational upward mobility has become increasingly tenuous.

Disruptive thinking may require us to step outside of our comfort zones and go to places that make us uncomfortable—or at least that make us shift our focus outside of ourselves. The T.D. Jakes Foundation partnered with Frito-Lay to send the entire Dallas public school system to see the Broadway play *Hamilton* when it came to Dallas. The school system had six weeks to prepare the kids, delving into everything about the play, from marketing to production to coding. I was so proud of these kids. Many people viewed them as "hoodrats," but what they wound up seeing instead were kids who were intelligent, respectful, and excited. To quote the play, these kids got to be in the room where it happens—and they stepped up. They just needed a chance. They needed for the adults to employ some disruptive thinking. They needed exposure. That's how you learn which fork to use. Exposure. Observation.

Once you have employed observation and communication, the final step is *integration*—learning how to use the information you have obtained from observation and communication and integrating it into your world view, thus directing your actions. That leads you to *transformation*.

To bring about the transformation we desperately need, we need you to be not only a disruptive thinker but also a disruptive doer. Find partners who can help you bring your vision to life. We are waiting for you to get it together. Time is not our friend.

FOUR

COLLABORATIVE SOLUTIONS

And straightway many were gathered together, insomuch that there was no room to receive them, no, not so much as about the door: and he preached the word unto them. And they come unto him, bringing one sick of the palsy, which was borne of four. And when they could not come nigh unto him for the press, they uncovered the roof where he was: and when they had broken it up, they let down the bed wherein the sick of the palsy lay. (Mark 2:2–4)

This biblical illustration is, in my mind, a great depiction of how we must seek to solve problems in a contemporary society that is facing complexities beyond human comparison. More and more, all sectors of our society are starting to realize that the final frontier of social justice includes an equity and inclusion component that has historically been ignored. What do we do about it? The powerful thrust of that question centers around the word *we* and not just the word *what*.

I am convinced more than ever that it will not be any one of us, but all of us working in a concerted cohesive effort to amass disruptive, transformative thinking. Philanthropy is a very important part of our society. It speaks to the empathy that one human has for another. It also expresses the goodwill of those who seek to serve the less fortunate. That's a fantastic human impulse. However, the reality is that needs have grown massive and continue to evolve post COVID-19 in a way that necessitates we develop a more holistic approach to solving problems and making a difference.

For the past twenty years, I have stood at the intersection between ministry and marketplace. I understood that ministry is incomplete without marketplace. Furthermore, as I begin to engage corporate leaders, I see that they have solutions but lack access to the people who could be recipients of those solutions.

It has been my wish to see bridges of hope built between sectors of society that traditionally do not engage each other for substantive change. For example, let me use the commonly expressed notion among people of faith that it is the church's job to take care of the less fortunate. In theory that is true, but in reality, that is impossible. We certainly bear a responsibility to participate in the process, but because the needs are massive, we cannot do it alone. Handing out turkeys at Thanksgiving and Christmas toys for children does not alleviate the suffering of underprivileged and homeless people. However, if we are able to provide job readiness, in addition to life, technological, and emotional skills, we could put our turkeys away. In order to accomplish this task, we at the church decided to set up several different entities that are not traditionally seen in church. United MegaCare, for example, is focused on disaster relief all over the world, meeting needs and providing clean water, clothing, shelter, or whatever we could to make a difference in the suffering of humanity. While the church is already a 501(c)(3), we decided that each charitable entity should have its own 501(c)(3) status, so that it would be able to access funds from other organizations and people who are interested in that entity's mission but, for whatever reason, may not want to support the church's message. The rules for such nonprofits depend on whether they are public foundations or privately held foundations. They require separate governing boards and the filing of an IRS form 990. It was very much like starting a company. Board-approved legal documents are required to outline how the entities engage with one another. It is an entrepreneurial-style struggle over the first few years getting to sustainability, but it works. We had to make the initial investment, organize benefits, and engage influencers and community leaders, but it's happening. Inch by inch we are carrying more people into the workforce and away from suicide, depression, and crime.

We had to solicit grants, funds, bonds, and investments that we wouldn't be eligible to receive as a church. This was done to stay afloat long enough to gather the empirical data that was necessary to chronicle the impact that larger donors seek prior to making an investment. A myriad of new grants and strategic partnerships are available if the corporate structure is done correctly.

The church had to support the other entities initially, but eventually help came with a proven record of integrity. Our multiple award-winning Texas Offenders Reentry Initiative (TORI) was started in a similar fashion. It took years of investing church and personal resources and engaging relationships outside of the church circle to successfully reduce the rate of recidivism, solicit employment opportunities, and find appropriate housing for nearly twenty thousand people who were trying to return to society. Make no mistake about it: this is not easy. However, it comes with the understanding that the problems we have are far too complicated for any one entity to resolve without a collaborative effort with others.

> *Bring ye all the tithes into the storehouse, that there may be meat in mine house, and prove me now herewith, saith the Lord of hosts, if I will not open you the windows of heaven, and pour you out a blessing, that there shall not be room enough to receive it. (Mal. 3:10)*

There were days I wondered if Malachi 3:10 might loosely be applied to those who refused to make room to receive these ex-offenders, because they had no interest in training and creating space for upward mobility. If the underserved and underrepresented elements of our community are to face an age of artificial intelligence, increasing technological gaps, and a constant decline in living-wage jobs, we will need to make sharp and immediate turns academically and socially to increase our capacity to be marketable. Otherwise, even the companies most focused on DEI issues will have opportunities that we don't have the capacity to receive.

What is also difficult is that most corporations have a strong aversion to if not skepticism of faith-based entities. I believe they subconsciously discriminate against us, failing to give equal access to opportunities that carefully selected faith-based leaders could utilize, which would result in a more equitable society. To discriminate against these churches, synagogues, or parishes on the basis of their faith and not on the basis of effective transformative results is, frankly, reprehensible. As a faith-based entity, we had to provide services far beyond the sphere of our faith. The masterful words of Christ warn us against giving a sermon when your brother needs a coat. A holistic, practical approach to ministry must pass out job applications and not just conversion cards. We serve anybody and everybody regardless of who they are as we seek to be a light of the world and not a candle in a church.

It is far easier to gain the engagement of elected officials and faith-based entities than it has been to get corporate support, but that is starting to change. Corporations are starting to realize that they have a lot to offer, but they can't buy trust. Many institutions like ours are a trusted voice in the community. No, not everyone trusts any institution anymore. But no one sees as many people of color on a weekly basis as houses of faith. The influence of the church in the Black community continues to rise, according to recent Barna Group research reports. Also, the church building itself is the most underutilized, highly expensive resource on the ledger of fiduciary responsibility in most communities, affording us the ability to host STEM programs, daycare for struggling mothers, food banks, and reentry programs—all accomplished through foundations and community development corporations.

Disruptive thinking asks, "How can we better utilize our facilities, staff, and influence to bridge the gap between services, suppliers, and recipients?" This question led to the development of the T.D. Jakes Foundation. I wanted to be sure that the missionary work we were doing in the community had its own identity and could exist between the community and the church more effectively. Many of the services that the foundation provides were already being done by the church, but they were not sustainable merely by tithes and offerings. In fact, if you took all the income from all of the churches in the United States and put it up against the budget that is needed for welfare, healthcare, eye care, transportation, groceries, utilities, rental assistance, and surgeries, it is obvious that you would run out of resources within sixty days. So, the notion that we could do it alone was a fantasy. Here's a disruptive thought for you: maybe churches could be connective tissue between government agencies, corporations, and community leaders and collectively do it together.

Because this has not been done before on any grand scale, it will take hours and hours of meetings, rearranging organizational constructs, and developing new models and templates for the corporations and the church. Nevertheless, we are living in a time when it is becoming increasingly clear that elected officials alone cannot solve our problems.

The Potter's House has several other entities—from real estate development, providing mixed-income housing, developing mixed-used communities, closing food deserts, and creating green spaces—that people have not seen really watching one of our broadcasts.

So, what can *you* do?

I suggest you start where you are with what you have, and make it available to serve who you can to the best of your ability until help comes. No one will help you if you remain in thought mode. You have to go beyond thinking it to doing it. Second, you must surround yourself with people who are relentless enough to carry a lame man up a wall and cut a hole in a roof to get him to what he needs. This kind of tenacity is the offspring of disruptive thinking. With agility, planning, straining, and determination, you can get there.

Let's start with vision. Developing an organizational construct that mirrors what you have in mind is a great place to start. Describe, investigate, and anticipate the obstacles that would hinder you from being successful. Great leaders anticipate obstacles. Clear the path and remove the brush between its present and its future.

I personally am not a great believer in setting up "doing business as" entities, because they do not provide enough protection against the assault on your personal assets should you run into a legal problem. Proceed with caution. The whole purpose of setting up a corporation is in part to ensure that you have created a firewall between you personally and what you seek to do. Your family will suffer enough without the problem of losing your home or car if something goes wrong. This legal firewall lessens the likelihood of you losing your personal assets in the process of trying to do good. Depending on what your vision is, you may need a 501(c)(3), a 501(c)(4), or an LLP for-profit company (whether it is an S or a C corporation depends on its function and the tax vulnerability that each entity creates). Do your homework first.

You may want to start a business, but if you're going to do that successfully, you want to build an organization that can hold your business at arm's length from your personal accounts.

I strongly urge a separate board of governance. I strongly urge that you include an accounting component. I strongly urge that you do not mix monies without paperwork to explain and validate who gave what to whom and under what terms. You really ought to get a lawyer if you're going to start a business, church, or foundation. It is important that you think about taxes, employees, and benefits. Any vision that you can accomplish by yourself is too small for you. Your organization should be a clear reflection of your vision, purpose, and goals.

I used Malachi 3:10 to start this dialogue because I do not believe that not-for-profits can fix the plight of our society unless they engage for-profit entities, elected officials, and faith-based leaders who are connected to community leaders. In that way, the equilibrium of lifting the weight of the downtrodden is equally dispersed between trusted community voices, corporations who want to give back, and elected officials who are necessary to make sure that what we are building complies with local governments and federal policies. Tax incentives, low-income tax credits, and assistance with infrastructure grants could help with housing; federal down-payment assistance for first-time homeowners exists but is poorly marketed. Only a little more than 40 percent of African Americans own their home, while rent is often more costly than a mortgage. There are vehicles out there already that can help right this listing ship.

Imagine if the man in the Bible who was sick of palsy had only three friends to lift him up. The balance would be broken. The sick man would be damaged, and the mission would be aborted. Disruptive thinking means that you are going to have to learn how to socialize, interact with, and fraternize with a diverse group of people in order to reach a common goal. We must attack these problems with much more than tweets. We must vote, organize, and work with those who see the impending crises, the dire need for housing, and the early death rates of pregnant Black women, and say enough is enough!

Nature itself teaches us that we don't have to be homogeneous in order to be fruitful. I can't afford to work only with people who look like me, believe like me, or vote like me. That's a privilege for the privileged. One doesn't interview an EMT in a car accident. We just strap down in the gurney with one goal: *Help me!*

Think a moment about reproduction. It is the story of opposites—when men and women get together, their differences complement each other, and their fruit becomes evidenced through the birthing of new life. The child is a product of their unity and their uniqueness. The cross-pollination among flowers, carried by bees, adds to the harvest time of the fruit of the trees. No one sits down to eat a meal that has no diversity on the plate. Everything around us is demanding that we get out of our comfort zones, leave our silos, step away from our comrades, and join the broader stream of society in order to provoke lasting change.

I have learned over the years that when all your associates are in your same field, do what you do, and know what you know, the only thing that can be born from the association is repetition, competition, or envy. I challenge you to get out of your comfort zone and into circles and spheres of influence that are built around what you do not do and do not duplicate what you already have accomplished. This man in the Bible surrounded himself with people who did not have the same weaknesses as he did. Consequently, he was able to be lifted, carried, and transported to a positive solution.

Building a team doesn't necessarily require a lot of money. Initially, building a team is merely a matter of developing a circle of like-minded people who are ready to explore innovative ideas, invest their time and energy, and share their contacts in the service of creating a path forward. For that matter, when you think about it, a family at its core is a team. I'm not necessarily suggesting that you make your family your business team. There are pros and cons to bringing your family into your business arena. Some family members can't handle it, and some may not be able to differentiate between who you are to them personally and who you are to them professionally. The worst part is that you could end up losing both relationships because of conflicts. However, theoretically, a team is composed of like-minded people with different skill sets but equal commitment toward measurable outcomes. It starts right there. It can be a team of volunteers. It can be a team that becomes a board. But each team member has to bring something to the table or, ultimately, they end up being resented at the table. Adorn your board with people who cover your limitations, not duplicate your strengths.

At the height of the COVID-19 pandemic I had the privilege of meeting Dr. Kizzmekia Corbett. She worked with the team of people that developed the vaccine that contributed to the diminishing of the deaths that were mounting at alarming rates in our country. I had an interesting interview with her where she explained that the preliminary process for creating the vaccine had existed for years. When the pandemic occurred, it was only a matter of enhancing what already had been developed to bring it to a point of fruition. We often refer to that as a straw man process in business. A straw man is not a finished product, but the preliminary development is in place and can be modified as details become solidified.

For a simple example, the "rough-in" stage during construction doesn't require knowing what draperies, carpets, or paint colors will ultimately go into the space. It is just a framework of what is next. If you make a substantial change to an existing contract, it is called a change order. However, the preliminary work has already been done in such a way that small changes and modifications need not be costly.

I am hoping that this book inspires you to at least lay the framework for what the next decade will look like for our world, for our community, and for our families. I am praying that it will inspire you to have the courage to disrupt the course you are on for the course you would like to see accomplished. Massive high-rise construction does not start with steel beams, concrete walls, expensive scaffolding, or glass windows. Massive construction starts with paper, pencils, and drafts. More recently we have forsaken the paper, pencils, and drafts for laptops and technology. Regardless of the change, transformation can be accomplished on a micro level without massive disruption. It starts on that level so that the disruption can occur within a controlled environment, minimize expenses, and maximize results.

Ultimately, Jesus commanded the man who was brought to him to social responsibility. Once we have done all we can do, everyone has to take personal responsibility. Jesus told the man, "Take up thy bed, and walk" (John 5:8). Can you imagine the anxiety brought about, the disruption he caused, the attention he drew, the silent stares of skepticism? I can almost hear his inner voices cackling like witches with long warts. *Suppose it doesn't work? What were you thinking?*

A self-doubting belief system creates mental and emotional atrophy. Could it be possible that life has more for him than this life sentence of incarceration imposed on him by an inescapable bed? The stiff spine crackles like dry cereal exposed to cold milk. Something is about to happen. His arms stretch, his hands clutch, his bedside awaits a change that will emancipate him forever. This could be the moment that changes all others. The chance of a lifetime is just past the turbulence of self-discovery. The guardrails are removed, encumbrances dismissed, boundaries eradicated. Even Jesus watches to see if his faith will not convert to works. A gasp goes through the crowd as the fifth man takes action.

When Jesus saw their faith, he said to the paralyzed man, "Son, your sins are forgiven." Now some teachers of the law were sitting there, thinking to themselves, "Why does this fellow talk like that? He's blaspheming! Who can forgive sins but God alone?" Immediately Jesus knew in his spirit that this was what they were thinking in their hearts, and he said to them, "Why are you thinking these things? Which is easier: to say to this paralyzed man, 'Your sins are forgiven,' or to say, 'Get up, take your mat and walk'? But I want you to know that the Son of Man has authority on earth to forgive sins." So, he said to the man, "I tell you, get up, take your mat and go home." He got up, took his mat and walked out in full view of them all. This amazed everyone and they praised God, saying, "We have never seen anything like this!" (Mark 2:5–12: niv)

Up until now, all the focus has been on the infusion of tenacity injected by the four men. The only question that remains rests solely on the fifth man, and he is proof positive that the journey the other embarked on is truly worth it.

Not every case will end in triumph. Many will slip backward and lie down again. But you can't ignore the conditions in our cities by rezoning, building more elevated highways, avoiding exit ramps, building higher walls, and hoping you'll be safe. You have to step up and engage.

I'm not discouraged. Instead, I'm grateful for people like John Lewis, Fannie Lou Hamer, Rosa Parks, Harry Belafonte, Dr. Martin Luther King Jr., George Floyd, Emmett Till, and countless others who have carried us to the wall. A few of us have scaled the wall and cut a hole in the ceiling. But many others are yet strapped to the gurney seeking the next generation of courageous people who will bear the weight to lift a dying society of women and Black and brown people who still await a chance to be carried to an equitable society. Can we do it? Yes, we can! But it will not be easy in this divisive society to get the breakthrough needed to achieve.

The only hope for your children and mine, for your generation and the next generation to come, for those who are yet strapped to the gurney, paralyzed and praying—the only way we can take up our bed and walk—is that we evolve to a collaborative solution. Then and only then can history record that ALL LIVES MATTER. I'm game. Are you?

FIVE

WHY DISRUPT?

When I was a relatively young man and had just started preaching on a national level, the *Washington Post* published a profile of me. I was used to appearing on Christian platforms, like the Trinity Broadcasting Network, the Christian Broadcasting Network, and *Charisma* magazine, but this was one of my first times in a national secular publication with a huge reach. The article said some nice things about me, but there were also parts of the story that weren't so nice. I was not pleased. In fact, I was quite raw after reading that piece. *I don't know if I want this*, I thought. *They don't even know me.*

I had to speak that night at Evangel Cathedral, where Apostle Donnie Meares is the lead pastor, in Upper Marlboro, Maryland. I decided that after I was done, I wasn't going to do any more speaking at that level, on that scale. I wasn't prepared to be evaluated by people who didn't know me and who would take little pieces of articles and make comparisons between me and people I didn't know. After I spoke that night, I went upstairs to the fellowship, but my heart wasn't in it. I was there and sort of not there at the same time. They told me there was a woman downstairs who wanted to see me—and she was willing to wait. I stayed upstairs as long as I could to avoid that woman. I knew I wasn't in the right headspace to be meeting with needy strangers.

When I went downstairs, I saw a woman standing there waiting for me. She was pale and looked weak and frail. This was the conversation as best as I can recall:

"I checked myself out of the hospital to come here," she said to me. "Because God told me to come hear you speak."

She now had my full attention.

"I lost my baby," she continued. "I had to carry a dead baby in my fallopian tube for months. I almost died."

She paused. "The only thing that kept me alive was hearing you preach."

She hesitated again. "It's hard for me to tell you this. The Lord sent me over here to tell you it's not for them that you do it. It's for us."

I was so stunned I could hardly speak. I thanked the woman, but I'm not even sure what I said to her. When I got in the car to go to my hotel, I started bawling. I cried all the way back to my hotel room. It was a moment of epiphany for me. I didn't start preaching for the *Washington Post*—what the heck was I thinking? For me, it was always about them, the people I serve, the community I grew up in. But somewhere in that barrage of media and attention, I had lost the point, the purpose. Ego had gotten in there and turned me all around. Yeah, they attacked me, but it was never about them in the first place. This woman had checked herself out of the hospital, barely able to walk, after carrying a dead baby inside of her, and she made her way to the church that night to remind me why I do it. And she said she had been sent by God. The timing of her message was unbelievable to me.

A few years ago, decades after that night in Upper Marlboro, I was at a signing for one of my books. The door swung open and a beautiful lady walked into the room to get her book signed. She came up to me.

"You don't know me, do you?" she said.

"No, ma'am, I don't think I do."

"I'm the lady that came to you at Donnie Meares's church," she said.

Immediately, I burst into tears. I leaped up from my chair and came around to hug her.

"You're the only reason that I made it," I said. "Because you reminded me why I do it. It's not for them—it's for us."

Success doesn't feel successful. That may sound counterintuitive, almost like an oxymoron, but hear me out. The biggest misconception people have about reaching what they would consider "success" is what it will feel like when they get there. We work our behinds off, toiling away in the dark of night, putting pleasure and family time on hold, all with the goal of getting to that magical place we have dreamed about. But when we get there, we quickly discover it's not the fantasy we had created in our heads. We find out there are all sorts of accoutrements—wanted and unwanted—that go along with success. There's a lot of pain, which steals away the savory satiety that we thought would greet us there. Success doesn't feel successful; it feels hard. It's not necessarily going to make us happy. It can be lonely. A lot of the sacrifices we made along the way come home to roost, with repercussions popping up in unexpected places, biting us in the behind.

I think the sacrifices we have to make are one of the biggest reasons success doesn't feel successful. We can't enjoy it because we have paid such a hefty tuition on our way there. We've reached the pinnacle, but now the bills are due. After we walk across the stage and are handed that degree, no matter how elaborate the graduation was, with Grandma crying and the aunties applauding and everybody taking us out to dinner and then partying with our friends later, one day that letter will come in the mail or it will hit our inbox telling us we owe $78,053.45. We were giddy to secure that job after graduation, but now we do the calculations and realize a $49,000 before-tax salary will be devastated by student loan payments. Success doesn't always feel successful.

Weddings are gloriously beautiful affairs, with an abundance of love and smiles flowing through the big reception hall. But after the dress gets stashed away, the work starts. It doesn't matter how lovely the wedding was; it's the marriage that counts.

The takeaway is this: we cannot pursue success for a feeling. If we're looking for elation or all-consuming joy, inevitably we will wind up disappointed. Crack addicts know the high only lasts for about five to ten minutes.[1] But the drug sends them on a desperate search for the next high, however fleeting it is. To me that sounds like torture.

At its best, success is much deeper than a feeling. Success probes more deeply than that: How did we impact the world? Did we make it a better place for other people? What difference did we make in exchange for the air we sucked up and the food we ate?

Before we leap over the fence, we must be clear on the reason we are pursuing the disruption. *Why disrupt?* Why are we making the leap? If we're doing it for a feeling, we'd be better off staying where we are and going to see a therapist. Leap in search of something more meaningful, a higher purpose. Success is not a fancy watch. It's not a tailored suit. It's not an impressive house. It's about that woman with the dead baby rotting in her fallopian tube preaching the greatest message I've ever heard in my life: it's not for them; it's for us.

Psychologists coined a term to describe the typical life span of the happiness derived from things that we buy: hedonistic adaptation. We anticipate the joy that the fancy new car we've been coveting will bring into our lives. We imagine the crisp smell of the leather seats, the thrill from the turbo thrust, the admiration of passersby when we pull up in the shiny new ride. When we actually purchase the dream car, we do indeed experience all of those pleasures. But in a few months, the thrill is gone, to quote B.B. King. We revert back to our baseline level of happiness. In fact, it also works in reverse: we usually stay sad for only a limited period after we experience loss or pain, then we revert back to our baseline. It's as if our brains understand that it would be dangerous to get too high or too low in response to external forces.

For disrupters, success may mean controversy. Success may mean death threats. Success may mean getting shot in front of a motel. Our history is abundant with examples of disrupters who paid the ultimate price after achieving a degree of success.

Like many others, I was emotionally devastated by the death of George Floyd. The sheer disgust of watching his body fluids run across the pavement after Derek Chauvin pressed the full weight of his body on Floyd's head will stay etched in my brain forever. But one of the most emotionally wrenching moments for me was seeing the video of his six-year-old daughter, Gianna, say, "Daddy changed the world!"

What a price to pay to change the world.

For Emmett Till, what a price to pay to change the world.

If we're striving for success for a feeling, we're going to be sorely disappointed. If we're doing it for the money, we're going to be disillusioned. Everybody wants to get paid for their work. I'm no different from the next man in that respect. But getting paid for it shouldn't be the reason we decide to do something disruptive. There has to be more to it than that. There has to be purpose. Isn't it curious that the employees who are happiest are those who feel fulfilled and content with their work, not the ones who make the most money? That should speak volumes.

Disruption should be about something bigger than ourselves. That's the only way we will weather the stormy days and nights. What older people know that young people don't is that you don't stay with a spouse for fifty years because they're sexy. Or because you have great chemistry in bed. Those things are seasonal. You stay with them for a lifetime because you've been sick together. You've been fools together. You've been poor together. You buried your parents together.

My wife and I often say that one of the secrets to our marriage is that we believe in something bigger than ourselves. We believed in our kids, in our family, in the good we could do in the world. Over the years, I have disappointed her; she has disappointed me. If all we believed in was ourselves, we wouldn't have made it.

We don't get married to endure pain and strife, but the pain and strife will come. We don't go to college to pay the tuition bill, but the bill has to be paid. Sometimes, paying the bill becomes the elephant in the middle of the room that we can't get beyond. We can't buy a house because we haven't been paying that student loan bill. We certainly weren't thinking about our future credit score when we walked across the stage to pick up that diploma. But nevertheless the tuition can't be avoided.

Can we afford the tuition of what's next? Is there a purpose that anesthetizes the pain we will encounter on our way to success? That purpose could be a child. It could be your mother. It could be getting out of the hood and all the harmful things that happened to you there. But it can't just be about buying the new house. I think Goliath was David's greatest blessing because he gave him something to kill. Had David not killed Goliath, Saul would never have paid him any attention, and he wouldn't have wound up entering into the palace. Goliath turned a delivery boy into a king. The gateway to every great "next" is a Goliath.

I don't get fulfillment out of lying on a beach for long stretches. After a week of sun, sand, and ocean breezes, I start getting antsy. What gets me out of bed in the morning is something to fight for and something to believe in and something to strive for. And I will jog for it. I will work out for it. I will do crazy stuff to get it. I get fulfillment from challenges. Great athletes like Michael Jordan and Tom Brady famously searched for enemies to get them motivated—if there wasn't one handy, they'd invent one.

When Jesus gathered with the disciples for the meal that would come to be called the Last Supper, he shocked them when he stood up, stripped off his outer clothing, wrapped a towel around his waist, and began washing his disciples' feet with water he had poured into a basin. He used the towel around his waist to dry their feet. Foot washing was a common practice before a meal in the time of Jesus, but it was something typically done by a servant. The disciples would never have considered washing each other's feet, let alone the feet of someone with lower status. But here was Jesus, the man they worshipped as the Son of God, kneeling down and washing their feet. This was the ultimate disruptive act—demonstrating that he was strong enough to be weak. He disrupted everything the disciples thought about leadership. He even washed the feet of Judas, although he knew Judas was about to betray him. Jesus fed his assailant and his detractors, understanding His purpose.

When Jesus got to Peter, Peter voiced what the others likely were thinking—that it wasn't appropriate for Jesus to wash their feet. Peter was used to seeing Jesus in the stereotypical way they would look at a leader. But Jesus told Peter, "Unless I wash you, you have no part with me" (John 13:8 NIV).

This is a beautiful story because it demonstrates disruption in the other direction—he was leading by being of service to them.

When he had finished washing their feet, he put on his clothes and returned to his place. "Do you understand what I have done for you?" he asked them. "You call me 'Teacher' and 'Lord,' and rightly so, for that is what I am. Now that I, your Lord and Teacher, have washed your feet, you also should wash one another's feet. I have set you an example that you should do as I have done for you. Very truly I tell you, no servant is greater than his master, nor is a messenger greater than the one who sent him. Now that you know these things, you will be blessed if you do them." (John 13:12–17 niv)

Jesus told his disciples that humble, self-sacrificing love shall be how people would recognize His followers.

A new command I give you: Love one another. As I have loved you, so you must love one another. By this everyone will know that you are my disciples, if you love one another. (John 13:34–35 niv)

I remember well a renowned friend, the late Bob Buford. In 1995, Bob Buford wrote *Halftime: Changing Your Game Plan from Success to Significance*, a popular book about how when some successful people realized that their lives had a lot of profit but no purpose, they wanted to spend the second half of their lives in service to others. In my travels, I've come across people like that—former doctors who walked away from medicine to become massage therapists, former CEOs who had started nonprofits. Their lives send a powerful message: sometimes the disruptive leap is across the fence in the other direction.

In many ways, this is the ultimate form of leadership, making yourself secondary to those who are following you.

It is role modeling in the extreme. I have tried to move in this way with many of the initiatives we have started through my church, my foundation, and my for-profit companies. The Texas Offenders Reentry Initiative is in that vein, as is the low- and moderate-income housing we are building through T.D. Jakes Real Estate Ventures.

Washing the feet of others may mean going back into the kinds of neighborhoods we escaped on our way to success. I realized we couldn't run TORI from the church; we had to put it where people had access to it. That meant seeing the place get burglarized before we realized we couldn't put nice furniture in there or fix it up too fancy. The people we seek to serve are not far enough along to accept success in their neighborhood without wanting to steal it and disrupt it and destroy it. In order to be redemptive, we have to become kin to the people we're trying to reach. We can't sit back in big offices and make big decisions about people we haven't met.

Jesus had always sat in the seat and had his feet washed, but this time he set aside his garments, kneeled, and looked up. To understand life from the other person's perspective means that you have to disrupt your norm to have a different experience. Scott Budnick was a hugely successful Hollywood producer whose credits include *The Hangover*, the highest-grossing R-rated comedy of all time, and its sequels. But in 2013, Budnick walked away from the big money and founded the Anti-Recidivism Coalition from his garage, helping former prisoners find jobs and homes and new lives. He also served as executive producer on the film *Just Mercy*, which highlighted the powerful, selfless work Bryan Stevenson has been doing with his Equal Justice Initiative in Alabama. Both Budnick and Stevenson are inspiring examples of men who have set aside their garments to serve others.

Washing the feet of others might bring us back into the community we were trying to escape, but sometimes the real challenge is to go where we've never been. Empathy is easy when it matches and validates our experience. But can you empathize with someone whose experience is very different? Oprah Winfrey built a girls' school in Soweto, a world away from her childhood home in Mississippi—though Oprah might say it didn't feel that far away at all. We are often made to feel guilty or responsible if we're not giving back to where we came from—but are we able to feel that same responsibility toward people who might not even look like us?

Jesus was asked in Luke 10, "Who is my neighbor?" That is such a powerful question for us all. Is my neighbor only the man I grew up with, listening to the same music, gobbling up the same bags of potato chips and Cheez Doodles? No. The man I don't know at all, the man who might be from a different community or part of the world, is still my brother. I'm not going to walk past him, see him destitute or homeless, and do nothing. I've never been to jail in my life, but I've run a prison reentry program for years. In doing service, we can't limit ourselves just to people we know and understand.

In fact, I think leadership is servitude. I don't believe you are a leader if you don't serve. Otherwise, what's the point? Good leadership is a service to humanity—not to ourselves. It's not about being allotted and applauded; it's about leveraging your influence to provoke some change, or to protect, or to prepare. In its truest form, leadership is service. We can't lose sight of that, though it can be easy to do in a society where everybody wants to rush to the front of the line. It's easy to become detached from those we seek to lead or to serve.

Of each one of you, I ask a simple question: Whose feet have you washed?

In the business realm, if your business solves a problem, customers will find you. If you have a dialysis business, you don't have to market it—they'll come because they have no choice. In the course of solving problems, you can be quite profitable. But the business has purpose, a mission. If you only serve yourself, you will eat alone. If you solve a problem and you serve somebody, your table will always be crowded. And that is disruptive. That's what separates great CEOs from poor CEOs, or great presidents from poor presidents—answering that clarion call to lay aside your garments. Mind you, serving doesn't always mean going into the neighborhood. It can also be about implementing policies that help the neighborhood. I think America is sick of people coming into repressed neighborhoods to do a photo op, make a speech, and disappear. I would rather you not come and solve a problem from afar.

Do you feel strong enough to be weak? Do you feel safe enough to be vulnerable? Are you secure enough in who you are to be able to forsake the façade of your garments, stop the camouflage, and serve somebody?

This question can be applied to marriage as well: Are you man enough to run a milk bath for your wife? Are you secure enough in who you are to put yourself out there for those you love—essentially, will you wash their feet?

As my kids were growing up, I worked hard not only to provide for them but also to buy them nice gifts. There were times when I had to put stuff on layaway because I couldn't buy it outright. But now that they're grown, they never mention any of the expensive gifts I bought them, the pianos, the vacations. What they valued most was the time I spent doing silly things with them that cost nothing. My daughter still talks about the day I took her to get some TCBY. I bought the girls cars when they were sixteen; I busted my butt to get those cars. They never mention those cars—they don't even know where they are. But they still remember when I brought them on a date to the Cheesecake Factory. Or when I turned the hose on them while washing the cars. Sometimes we're working hard to give people things because we think that everything is about capitalism, about accumulating stuff. But the real move is not about that. It's about giving your time and attention. Those are the modern corollaries of foot washing.

Are you willing to lay aside these five things to serve?

1. **Time.** This is such a precious commodity; putting it aside speaks volumes.

2. **Title.** This means coming in the form of a servant, not a master. Dropping your PhD and serving beans and potato salad with the rest of us. Not hiding behind your massive accomplishments, your Oscar, your own version of an Oscar—whatever you're extremely proud of. Can you risk laying that aside?

3. **Talent.** Okay, you might be able to run the whole agency, but are you willing to mentor, expose people to creative influence, give your talent away to the dreams and aspirations of more than self-aggrandizement?

4. **Treasure.** Yes, this one is about money. No investment means no return. It's going to cost something to do anything truly impactful.

5. **Temperament.** Are you willing to risk managing your emotions differently to make yourself available for people who don't normally fit the profile of the people you like to be around? Possessing the emotional maturity to manage moods, opinions, and preferences of personality types for the greater good is essential. People who don't can't grow with you.

The temperament that we need to survive in the hood is not the temperament that we need to survive in a workplace—though they are both jungles and they both have predators and evil-doers. We must be able to adapt, to bend when and where necessary. We might have a PhD and on the surface appear to be ideally suited for corporate America, but if our temperament hasn't caught up to our degrees, we might still be apt to act a fool when somebody makes us angry.

In certain situations, we may need to lay aside our garments to serve. I could take you into prison with me; you would not be well-advised to go in there and tell everyone that you have a PhD. They don't care about that. You would do much better to go in there in ripped jeans and a T-shirt, saying, "Yo, what's up, man? How you doin'?" You're telling them, *I came to check on you. I came to care.* Not everybody can lay aside what they are proud of. But it may be necessary for you to be relevant to people who are in pain. Connection is the key to communication. We must be able to tailor our presentation to our audience. The same language and demeanor won't be effective both on a university stage and in the barbershop. Orators are not great because they are eloquent; they are great because they're effective. If the ear of the listener was unable to receive the orator, that orator was not effective. We must be willing to jump the fence to forge the connection that will make us effective. When I go to Mexico, I try to speak Spanish even though I don't speak it well. My attempt opens doors for me because it says to them, *Oh, you're trying to acknowledge me. You respect our language and our culture.*

I have a final word of warning about the collateral effects of the kind of success we might find when we jump the fence: success can cast a shadow. When we get attacked as a result of being a disruptive thinker, that blowback doesn't just land on us; it can victimize the people we love—our children, our family, our friends. Whether they're littles ones in diapers or elders on a pension, they didn't choose to be victimized. But we have to cope in an environment that includes a myriad of reactions, both positive and negative. Get your loved ones, your people, your friends prepared.

Success casts a shadow because the kids are expected to live up to the level of their predecessors. Many of them thrive in the crucible of that kind of pressure. Imagine what it feels like to be the children of Colin Powell, or Toni Morrison, or Nelson Mandela. They must find their way through the fog of their father's or mother's brilliance. That's a pretty long shadow that they'll spend much of their lives trying to crawl out from under.

And if their parents have moved from fame to infamy, what then? How hard is it to be the child of Bill Cosby or O.J.

Simpson? The shadow is something you didn't ask for, but you still have to figure out how to deal with it. Disrupters must consider how the disruption will affect the kids—because in many cases the pressure can break them. The same sun melts the wax and hardens the clay. It depends on the material the sun hits. There is definitely going to be a reaction either way. Sometimes you can have both reactions in the same house, working with the same DNA—melting here and hardening there.

There's an amusing adage that touches on this idea. When the town alcoholic got a woman pregnant, she gave birth to twins. One twin declared, "I never drink." When he was asked why, he said, "Because my father was an alcoholic." But the other twin? He was found stumbling around the park, clearly drunk. He was asked why he drank so much. He said, "Because my father was an alcoholic." The exposure we get growing up can be an asset or a liability. It's up to us to decide which one.

My brother once told me that when we were in West Virginia, he had a name. "But when we came to Dallas, I became T.D. Jakes's brother." He had to struggle to get out from under my shadow. This spirit is going to affect the people around us, whether they are disrupters themselves or not. They will find the spotlight even when they don't want it. If they make a mistake, now it's a news story. If it was somebody else's child or sibling, it wouldn't be a story. Now your divorce is news—you're being sued and your ex is getting an interview. Because *you* are deemed important.

Psalm 91:1 says, "He that dwelleth in the secret place of the most High shall abide under the shadow of the Almighty." That's meant to be comforting, to be shelter. But then we get Psalm 23:4. "Yea, though I walk through the valley of the shadow of death, I will fear no evil: for thou art with me; thy rod and thy staff they comfort me." That's not meant to be comforting—that's threatening, looming, intimidating. *Shadow* is used in both places, but the meaning has quite a different effect. Both experiences occur, depending on the person, their resilience, and their ability to manage something that they didn't even choose. That's true in any walk of life. For preacher's kids, sharing their father or mother with a mass of people is not easy. But the shadow doesn't stop at the cathedral. That shadow moves out and across the lawn of a university to a top professor; it spreads down to the local ER to a hot-shot surgeon. Can you imagine running the cash register at the Walmart and your mother is a recipient of a Nobel Prize? Are you any less a person because you didn't go the way she went? Of course not, but you're going to feel the coldness of that shadow at the Thanksgiving dinner, or when her colleagues come over to the house. "So, Kathy, what are you up to these days?" The question is going to come; you can't hide from it forever.

Disrupters must brace the people around them to know scrutiny might be coming. The shadow will always be on their heels. A young man called me the other day and said, "I'm thinking of running for office."

I said, "Good. What does your wife think? What does your daughter think? Can your daughter handle it? Can she deal with what they're gonna say about you—for the next six months on the front page of the paper? In negative ads on television? Have you talked to your mother?"

These discussions can be quite delicate. You opened a successful hardware store, and you intend to pass it on to your son. But that's not in his mind—he wants to do hip-hop. You're trying to cram a hardware store into the mouth of someone who's in his room writing rhymes. Every time you look at him, he sees disappointment in your eyes because he wasn't what you had in mind. That disappointment reaches him deep down in his gut—saddening him, angering him, disappointing him. You're killing it at the store, but when you get home you feel like a failure because the relationship with your son has deteriorated. Your metrics of success don't include your son doing what he wants to do—he has to be what you have always dreamed that he would be. There's no room for him to be himself.

If you're struggling with the burden of expectations for your children, you might consider this thought: Your love has to be unconditional, or it won't survive this. Your love can't be predicated upon your children duplicating you, imitating you, succeeding you. Your love must be large enough, wide enough, for the kids to have space to explore who they are without worrying about your approval.

If you're dealing with expectations for your spouse, you should remember what brought you two together. It wasn't about what you do, but who you both are. You didn't marry what he does, you married who he is. You've risen to CEO, but he's a short order cook at a Dew Drop Inn restaurant—and you're reluctant to introduce him at the country club. You love him at home, but you're embarrassed by him in public. If your ego cannot accommodate who he truly is, then you either have to change who you're going to love—because they will always be frozen under that shadow—or you will need to reconsider how important disruption is to you. Many have walked away from a spouse because they chose their career over the partner. But others have chosen the love over the impressive career.

Ground rules need to be set at the beginning. What brought us together? Why am I important to you? What about me do you love? And how will that be affected as you pursue your dream and I pursue mine—though mine might not be as grand as yours? Couples need to have some uneasy conversations if they're going to survive the upheaval that can come when one of them is leaping over the fence and the other is not.

In families, in relationships, everybody is going to disappoint everybody at some point before the movie is over. Is your love strong enough to accommodate disappointment? And who gave you the right to plot the course of the rest of my life? At some point on that road, the spouse is going to tell you that your dreams and their dreams aren't compatible. Or the child is going to rise up and tell you, "I'm my own person—I'm not you—and you don't get to plan my life out." The child might throw your own past back in your face, pointing out that you did some stupid stuff along the way and made questionable decisions, so you need to step back. That's the painful material of life, and none of us can avoid it. If you can't go through that and find that your love is stronger than your disappointment, then that family will go bankrupt and you'll start another one. Disappointment is an equal opportunity employer. None of us escapes.

Every relationship, whether it's with a wife, husband, son, or daughter, will have these aggressive, sometimes attacking, conversations that trigger your pain, rage, insecurity, frustration, and control. Family is the gymnasium God created for love to work out in. We get the whole bundle: resistance training, sweating, pulling weights, pushing, tugging. Love works out first in the family. What does your gym look like?

You don't have to leave to leave. You don't have to divorce to divorce. You don't have to quit to quit. You don't have to move to be an absentee father. You can just become a workaholic and not be available. *Oh, I have to go to a meeting. Again.* We have a thousand ways to quit, but only one way to win: to relentlessly, tenaciously pursue a path forward while holding tight to your loved ones and also giving them space. It's not easy, but that's the only way to win.

SIX

WHY IT'S SO DIFFICULT

They were so alike, but yet so different. And we love them both.

Bentley—who is no longer alive—was jet-black and barrel-chested, strong and loyal. Honey is a bit smaller, the color of a jar of rich, sweet honey—and imbued with the feisty spirit of a revolutionary. They are Cane Corsos, a large, muscular dog breed known for its noble bearing and intimidating demeanor—what you'd want in a bodyguard, as reflected in their name, which roughly translates from Latin as "bodyguard dog." Bentley and Honey have been cherished members of the Jakes family and have taught me many things.

Where we live in Texas is quite rural—lots of farmland populated with livestock and fields of vegetation, but also an unnerving number of coyotes and poisonous snakes. We've lost a few dogs in the past, killed by the copperheads that lurk outside our property. I didn't want Bentley and Honey to meet the same fate, so we installed an invisible electronic fence system that would deliver a shock to the dogs if they tried to venture beyond the fence. The fence is there to protect them.

The dogs had radically different reactions to the fence. Bentley kindly acknowledged the boundaries and had no interest in trying to breach them. Honey hates the fence—she treats it like we are jailers trying to keep her on lockdown. She does not see the fence as her friend at all. Honey will brush off the pain of the shock, scoff at the sting, to get to the other side. Whatever she sees out there in the beyond, Honey considers it worth the pain—like Denzel taking the lash in *Glory*.

I talked in previous chapters about how disrupters decide they are willing to jump the fence and deal with the consequences. This "fence" I speak of isn't just an abstract metaphor—I'm really thinking about Honey and Bentley. Two dogs of the same breed, in the same household, under the same circumstances with two vastly different reactions. Just like humans, who all have different reactions to the fences in our lives. Some of us are willing to leap, no matter the consequences. Many others will stay comfortably inside that fence. Others will sit tight inside the fence but might be yearning to leap over it.

In American cities, there are fences all over the place. Fences built by race, fences built by socioeconomic levels, fences built by culture. Incidental fences and intentional fences. After the passage of the Federal-Aid Highway Act of 1956, many federal and state highway builders purposely chose Black communities as the sites for massive highway projects—destroying thriving centers of Black life in the process. Interstate 94 in St. Paul, Minnesota, displaced one-seventh of the city's Black residents. Interstate 579 in Pittsburgh demolished the Black community known as the Hill District. Interstate 4 in Orlando created a barrier separating the Black community from the east side's central business district and white communities. In Miami, the construction of Interstate 95 devastated the Black community called Overtown, such a prosperous center of Black economic and cultural life that it was known as the "Harlem of the South"—until it virtually disappeared, like it was never there. In all these instances, fences were constructed to constrain or to crush.[1]

We also have invisible fences in our homes. A woman who remains in a home with an abusive husband is constrained by a psychological fence. Her abuser builds the fence to separate her from her family, telling her that nobody loves her and cares about her but him. Little by little, the abuser has isolated her and confined her, so much so that he can go to work and know she'll still be there when he returns.

When Patty Hearst, heiress to the Hearst media empire, was kidnapped at gunpoint in 1974, she elicited the sympathy of the nation. But less than three months later, Hearst was toting a machine gun and helping her captors, the revolutionary Symbionese Liberation Army, rob a bank while pledging her allegiance to them. It was a classic case of a condition psychologists had termed Stockholm syndrome, named after four Swedish bank workers who were held hostage for six days and came to side with their captors. The mind is a fragile piece of work, susceptible to manipulation and mistreatment.

The reality is that we all have invisible fences in our lives, quietly working to hold us back, to make us afraid, to curtail our attempts at boldness. To stop us from being disruptive. In chapter 2 I talked about the time when I screamed at the TV set because I saw a young man say he was trapped in his neighborhood. I said that he could escape his circumstances—he could be poor anywhere in America, even on the beach. My response was logical, but what I failed to do was to recognize his invisible fence. There was something keeping him in that community that I couldn't see from my comfortable couch.

When you were growing up, did someone tell you that you were stupid, or ugly, or goofy, or awkward? Or that you were shy or lazy? Or your nose is too wide? Or your ears are too big? Have those words established a permanent home in your psyche, where they have been living rent-free for twenty or thirty years or more, chipping away at your self-esteem, making you timid and uncertain? The fears and insecurities that we carry around with us are invisible fences, carefully constructed and reinforced by the negativity of others, woven together to form an intimidating barbed-wire barrier that continues to imprison us.

The people who directed the negativity at us weren't always speaking with the intention to hurt us. Unfortunately, it is a basic trait of us humans to want to be better than the person next to us. This may be especially potent in oppressed communities that have long been subjected to economic, psychological, and even physical abuse. The need for power, for dominion, is extremely seductive—and another type of insecurity. There's a thin line between the victim and the perpetrator. The person who creates the system needs to have control, often because at one point in their lives things were out of control, or because they were the victim. They cling to any shred of power they can find—even if it comes at the expense of a family member or a spouse they actually love.

In the Scriptures, when two men go to Jesus' priests to confess, one cries, "Woe is me, for I am a terrible sinner." The other man says, "Thank God I am better than him" (Luke 18:10–13).

Feeling better than the other stops us from admitting we are bad, flawed. When they directed negativity at you, what they were really doing was finding a way to avoid looking inward and doing a self-assessment. It probably wasn't about you at all.

It is important to point out that my dogs Honey and Bentley did not construct their own electronic fence. That fence was built by someone else and forced upon them. The same actuality applies to our invisible fences. For the most part, we did not build them ourselves; they were forced upon us. Think about your own life—who built your fence? Was it the neighborhood? Was it a parent or grandparent? Was it a sibling? Was it a first grade teacher? Was it early child molestation?

No matter our background, race, or socioeconomic class, we all have fences to jump. In order to jump them successfully, we need to figure out what they are built of. Fear? Insecurity? Intimidation? Is it because everybody else in the family got a degree but you? Is it because everybody else in the family is more attractive than you are, or lighter, or skinnier, or smarter? Knowing what your fence is made of determines how high you have to climb or to jump in order to get over it. Is the voice within or is it without? Is it an external force such as the sociological system that keeps some of us poor, or the interstate that destroyed our community, or the educational system that fails to prepare us to thrive in mainstream society? Or is it internal—an inner voice that is chaining us to this spot and preventing us from leaping?

For me, the fact that I was a Black boy in a "colored" neighborhood in West Virginia, a state where the Black population was just 5 percent, was an external factor that constructed my fence. Looking inward, I built my own fence with my perception that my older brother was superior because he was an athlete like my father and I was not. One of the ways that I began to deconstruct my fences—and all of them are still not deconstructed, to be honest—was to develop an appreciation for what my strengths were. My father was nice to me, but he wasn't enthralled by writing or playing the piano. He was enthralled by touchdowns, basketball, hard work, and commitment. My mother, on the other hand, as an educator was more impressed the more articulate you were, the more prolific you were, the more immersed you were in the arts and finance. When I turned six, my mother gave me a bank passbook for my own savings account as a birthday present. We got to go to the bank to set it up. I was so proud of that passbook. I had maybe $50 in there, and I thought it was amazing.

I was caught between these two value systems—one in which I'm applauded, and the other in which I'm patted on the head but not understood. Admired in one, tolerated in the other.

To deconstruct my fences, I had to go back and delve into what built them in the first place. I grew up as a child of the civil rights movement, but I was incubated in the safety of my own house, so my blackness didn't feel like a fence when I was younger. Even though my father didn't understand me, I felt like the golden child in my mother's gaze. I had insecurities, but I had love and even adoration.

Understanding our fences and deconstructing them is so crucial to moving forward. We can't have construction without deconstruction. Even if the land is flat, you still have to destroy the land to put in an infrastructure that allows you to build upward. The people who broke the rules, who took the risks, who walked into the rooms where they were underestimated, who crossed professions, who achieved not just riches but fulfillment in marriage and family and home ownership and anything meaningful, likely had both outer and inner fences that they needed to leap across to get there.

Jesus certainly jumped over his share of fences. The reason the Pharisees and the Sadducees—the ruling class of Jews in Israel—both hated Jesus was because He didn't fit in the yard. The reason the high priest consented to conspire to have Him executed is because He threatened their power. He wouldn't follow their rules. He knocked over tables. He ate corn on the Sabbath. He healed people He wasn't supposed to heal. To be like Jesus, you had to be a fence jumper. However, it's important to note that Jesus did not jump the fence without a strategy.

Once we decide to jump, we need to have a strategy to survive and thrive on the other side. Where do I stay? What happens when there's no food left—how will I eat? To make the jump worthwhile, it has to be sustainable. Many of us aren't taught to think about sustainability; we are taught to get the immediate gratification of looking like we have jumped the fence. We buy beautiful cars and park them in front of cheap houses. We wear brand-name clothes but have no life insurance or health insurance. Because we're desperately in need of feeling exceptional, of wanting to signal to people that we have jumped the fence.

When I was a young man, I only had one suit to my name. When I was dating Serita, they called me One Suit Jakes. After I lost my job, I couldn't afford to get the suit cleaned anymore, so Serita put my suit in the washing machine until the lining fell out. To this day, I have trouble unbuttoning my suit jacket because I got so accustomed to keeping it closed to conceal the fact that it had no lining. The fence is still there decades later, living in my head without paying rent. I developed a thing for buying new suits because I was still haunted by One Suit Jakes. I don't even want to admit how many suits I have now. Still fighting that fence.

When we go to therapists to try to deconstruct our fences, we first have to figure out what they are and where they came from. It's a vital process. But only about 19 percent of American adults see a therapist in a typical year. The number is even lower for African Americans and Hispanics, at about 13 percent.[2] That means too many of us are walking around with no clear idea of what is holding us back.

We're never hungry for what we were full of; we're hungry for what we didn't get. If you were full of food growing up, having an overflowing plate is no big deal now. But if you were hungry all your life, you eat insatiably now. I learned that lesson with my five children, who have taught me so many things. When I was growing up, my parents would start preparing the Christmas meal days before the holiday actually arrived. It was by far the biggest meal of the year, a delectable smorgasbord that would overwhelm the entire table with dishes that seemed to go on forever. I was eager to continue that tradition in my own home when my children were growing up. I would start cooking three days before Christmas, preparing every dish imaginable. In my mind, I was providing them with a memorable holiday tradition that they might continue in their own families.

But one year, we sat down at the table for a wonderful family meal, and later that afternoon I looked up and saw my kids coming back into the house carrying bags. McDonald's bags. On Christmas Day, they had gone out and gotten food from McDonald's. I was floored. Talk about sacrilege—for a second I wondered if I could get away with throttling my own children. Over three days I had made every type of homemade bread, cinnamon rolls, pies, cakes, stuffing, greens, green beans, casseroles, Jell-O molds. Every food imaginable was sitting in the refrigerator—and they went to McDonald's? I exploded in anger.

"Do you know how hard I work to cook this food and make things amazing for you?!"

They all stared at me. One of them finally said, "Dad, we're PKs [preacher's kids]. We've had food all our lives. We've been inundated with desserts—people are always baking us cakes and pies and all kinds of stuff. Food is not important to us."

Wow. I had to sit down to absorb what they were saying to me. Full of humility, I looked at them and asked, "What would be a great Christmas to you?"

Their answer devastated me: "The greatest Christmas we could have would be to have you to ourselves."

Serita and I had been so busy giving them what we didn't get that we didn't give them us. In preparing the lavish Christmas spread, I was feeding that little boy in West Virginia eating government cheese and drinking WIC milk. That little boy walking up the hill with my mother after catching the bus to the grocery store. That's who I was sweating in the kitchen to feed. It was my point of reference, not theirs.

After that scene, I stopped all the cooking for Christmas. Instead, we went away for Christmas so they could have us to themselves. We played in the pool and did family activities and had a fabulous time. That became our new Christmas tradition. I began to understand that I needed to raise a child I could never have imagined, rather than raising a child that I was. I hadn't even been aware of how my childhood of scarcity remained an invisible fence in my head.

Do you still have a fence up there that you're leaping over when you buy that new house or that fancy car or push to get yet another degree? Are you ready to deconstruct that fence, to tear it down so that you can free yourself from its covert grip?

I once counseled a flasher—a guy who would go to highways and busy streets and open his coat to show passersby all that God gave him. I suppose I helped this man, but in actuality working with him was a profound learning experience for me. I told him, "I'm not here to judge what you do. I want you to tell me *why* you do what you do."

He said, "When I go out on the highway and flash people who drive by, they see me. And it gives me an erection."

"Why is that?" I asked.

His face turned red and tears began flowing down his cheeks.

"My mother told me I was a mistake. All my life she told me she regretted having me. She never saw me. And the feeling that somebody sees me is the sexiest feeling I've ever had in my life."

I didn't condone his behavior, but I understood it. I've counseled killers on death row, and we go through the same process. Deconstructing their fences. Understanding why. We spend so much time anesthetizing the pain of events that we never take time to go back and understand the why. We can't deconstruct what we don't understand. In Genesis 25:21–22, when Rebekah is pregnant with the twins Jacob and Esau and they are causing great agitation in her womb, she asks, "Why am I thus?" This is such a profound question to which we all can relate. It gets to that fundamental interrogation: *Why?*

Why does it scare me to walk into a room full of people who look different from me?

Why do I have the education to get a job that makes me uncomfortable in the room it put me in?

Why am I fifty years old trying to prove I'm still a stud?

Why am I angry?

If a man usurps authority and doesn't respect my mind, why do I attack him? Who am I really talking to?

I counseled a couple that had just gone through an episode where the wife went ballistic on him, yelling and fussing. I told him, "She's not even talking to you. She's talking to somebody before you. And you're walking around here bleeding from what she said."

In our culture we spend far too much time devouring the what of events, of controversies, of despicable behavior, without exploring the why of the story. Why was the fence built? Even if it was well intended, it's still confining us, directing our actions, making us afraid or angry or jealous. I didn't build the fence to hurt my dogs or to limit their movement; I built the fence to save them from getting killed. My intentions were pure. But they didn't see it that way.

Too often, we sit back and wait for the person who built the fence to take it down. That's not how that fence is going to be deconstructed. What happens if they die? What happens if they never take it down? Will we never escape its effects? Will we wait our entire lives?

African Americans are often celebrated for being the "first Black" this or that. Somehow, at this late date, we still see "first Black" people popping up in virtually every field. But while we applaud that accomplishment—perhaps with a bit of dismay—we don't often consider the burden that being the "first Black" places on us, the brand-new fence it is constructing in our heads.

Being the first is something we're rightly proud of—we'll blast it out on our bios, our resumes, our social media pages. But it's the classic case of the double-edged sword. Because while it's usually a clear sign that we have done well for ourselves—we have probably jumped quite a few fences to get there—the honor also means every time we walk out our front door, we carry the weight of 40 million people with us. Suppose we fall? Does that mean every African American in the country has fallen, too? If I'm the first Black CEO of the hospital, am I dishonoring all of my people if I get a DUI? Have I made it likely that the hospital will never again put a Black person in the CEO suite? To borrow from a popular song, every step we take, every decision we make, we feel like they're all watching us.

Kamala Harris isn't just the vice president of the United States; she's the first female, first Black, and first Asian American vice president. She's representing all those groups in everything she does, and all those who come behind her will be measured with a yardstick that she didn't ask for. When I was younger, they used the term "credit to your race"; that term isn't in use any more, but the idea and the pressure still applies.

When I received my first NAACP Image Award, I said in my acceptance speech that I've received a lot of accolades and honors, but to have your own people clap for you is utterly intoxicating. It suggests that I did you proud; it's almost the way a child feels when he has done something to please his parents. But there's always the flip side—the shame that child feels when he has embarrassed or dishonored his parents. When we are "the first," it can feel like we have 40 million parents watching over us. The weight of that is almost cruel—like we have been installed into a public office that we didn't run for. That weight can keep us up at night, staring at the ceiling, riddled with anxiety. That weight creates alcoholism, substance abuse, alienation, porn addiction—anything that helps us escape from the terror of outrunning the herd.

I have many close friends who have done exceptional things in their lives and risen to amazing heights. We all love each other, but we don't get to see each other often enough because we're all so busy, jumping on and off planes, trying not to fall off a cliff. When we do get together, it's a weighty time for us because we can let down our guard and be vulnerable. I had a dude who is president of a global company sitting at my dinner table, and I didn't ask him any questions about how his company is doing, what his shareholders are saying, what his bottom line is looking like. The question I asked him was simple: "How are *you*?" At my table with fourteen people sitting there, he burst into tears, and I had to take him out of the room. We wound up talking until midnight, being open and honest, helping each other cope. We are the minority of a minority—too white to fit in your Blackness, too Black to fit into their whiteness. At least that's our perception. When we get around our brothers, we hear, "Oh, I knew you when! Look at you, a college professor now! A big shot!" It's a joke— but it ain't. When that same professor is around his academic colleagues, he gets a lot of patronizing pats on the back. "Oh, we're so glad to have you here . . ." As if they had to have a special meeting to decide to do something as off-the-wall as hiring a Black professor—and he should feel grateful.

In Psalm 142, David expressed his anguish when he was alone in the cave: "I looked on my right hand, and beheld, but there was no man that would know me: refuge failed me; no man cared for my soul" (v. 4). That scripture reflects the loneliness many of us feel when we're caught between these two polarities. I sometimes feel it when I'm toiling away on groundbreaking deals. I recently closed a deal with Amazon that put three hundred of my messages into the homes of 186 million people, the first person of faith ever to do such a deal. I closed a deal with Roc Nation, and it became the first gospel project to make a deal with them on that scale. I closed a deal with Wells Fargo that is building homes for low- and moderate-income families in cities across America— something that Wells Fargo has never done before. I know what these deals represent—and the magnitude of that can be profoundly unsettling. *Why did God give this to me?* It's all so terrifying, it doesn't even feel rewarding. I'm too busy trying to close every door, shut every window, and pull every blind to get pleasure from it. Maybe that will come later. I sure hope so.

Every time I've done a first deal, I represent all of my faith, or all of my race, or all of my gender, or all of my Jakesness. I'm walking into the room with my ancestors every time, feeling like if I fall, they all go down with me. It's a feeling that so many of us have when we are walking that achievement high wire. Can't mess this up. Can't take a day off. Can't let them catch me slipping. Can't let them catch any of us—any of the hundreds or thousands who are working with me behind the scenes—slipping. Man, I'm sweating just reading these words back.

One of the things they don't tell us about the other side of the fence is how hard it's likely going to be to feel comfortable there. We've gotten the degree and we're certainly qualified for the job, but now we have to figure out the culture of this new world. Because the culture of an organization is never in the employee manual. We have to become adept at reading the tea leaves and sifting through the meaning of side conversations and off-the-cuff comments. In order to be accepted, we might have to let go of our native tongue—because there's no greater conversation stopper than that articulate, bright, young Black man getting pissed at somebody and calling him calling him something inappropriate We have to be able to know that they're playing us and not act on it, which is extremely hard for many of us. But those are the rules on the corporate playing field.

When I was working with these large companies to convince them to give jobs to ex-offenders as part of the Texas Offenders Reentry Initiative, I expended a lot of sweat clearing a pathway for them in corporations that weren't immediately enthusiastic. But it was a core value for us, to be a bridge builder between underserved populations and corporate America. However, I failed to consider what this all looked like from the other side of the fence. When I brought a group of the ex-offenders out to dinner, I exhorted them to make the best of the opportunity, to step into these companies and show that they could thrive. But as I looked around the table, the realization hit me like a punch in the stomach: they were terrified. I had underestimated how horrified somebody who grew up in the hood and spent the last seven years in jail would feel about walking into a room full of educated, successful white people. I overlooked the trauma of feeling like you don't belong in the room.

This idea of finding ways to fit into new spaces can't be overemphasized. That's what is so amazing about the story of Folorunso Alakija. She started out as a secretary in her native Nigeria, then decided to pursue her passion for fashion and went to study fashion design in London. Within a few years, her Rose of Sharon House of Fashion became a household name in Nigeria. But she didn't stop there. She bought an oil conservatory in Nigeria in the middle of the water that nobody thought was worth much—until she hit oil. Now Alakija is a billionaire, and one of the richest Black women in the world. What Oprah is to the US, Alakija is to Nigeria. When I've sat down with her, she has been frank with me about the obstacles she encountered. To go from the safety of just being responsible for typing a letter to a runway in Paris is gutsy as hell—and terrifying. However, having guts wasn't enough to get her there. She had to go back to school and train for that. She had to combine chutzpah with her education, and she had to keep pushing even when it was scary on the other side of that fence.

We tell our kids to go get the degree, and that's a wonderful, important thing. But we fail them if we don't give them the courage to leap that fence. The obstacles they're going to encounter can drive their degree all the way back to your house. It's not what you learn; it's what your parents or your DNA or your pastor or somebody put in you—that fire burning inside of you, torching your belly. The roar of the lion is more lethal than the lion's teeth, because the roar is what makes us soil our pants. That woman who got the degree but left corporate America to raise her kids is afraid of what she doesn't know when she walks back into the office. She's gotten great at being a soccer mom, making sure the team practices and games are a well-oiled machine, but what the hell is all this technology gibberish they are expecting her to master? Now she's having to make a presentation with a degree she hasn't used in twenty years.

A brilliant guy works with me now after running banks and killing it in corporate America. When he got ready to apply for a crucial license we needed to move our business forward—something he has done dozens of times before—he was at a loss for how to do it because the process is now online. We were held up for two weeks because he didn't want to tell us he didn't know how to use the technology.

No matter how experienced and educated you are, if you haven't been on the field for a while, you're going to have to relearn the game. Athletes know this instinctively. Everything is moving so fast, you blink and you get left behind. When I was in my early twenties working for Union Carbide, I didn't think twice about jumping into an eighteen-wheeler and moving it across the lot if it needed to be moved. I couldn't ride a bike, but I learned to drive an eighteen-wheeler—this stuff doesn't always make sense. Nearly thirty years later, when I was about fifty, I was asked to drive an eighteen-wheeler in a commercial. I guess they figured it would be a compelling sight for people to see Bishop Jakes behind the wheel. *No problem*, I thought. *I got this*. It was an opportunity for me to show off my blue-collar pedigree.

But when I jumped in the rig and got behind the wheel, I looked down and was alarmed by what I saw. Everything had changed; it looked nothing like I remembered. It was so automated, I could have been driving my own car. I sat there trying to figure it out while the whole crew waited.

If you've been away for a while raising your children or going to school or doing any number of productive things, you come back in as a minority—no matter if you're Black, white, or brown. When a white woman who's gotten a divorce and is now reentering the workforce walks into the office on her first day, she's Black scared. She shares the same terror that African Americans in corporate America have been confronting for decades.

When I was the pastor of a small storefront church in West Virginia, a white lady came to my church one Sunday and said she had watched me on TV. She had traveled to Charleston to find my church.

"Can white people come to this church?" she asked me.

I was astounded. I thought, *Y'all can go anywhere you want to go*. But that was my Black perception talking. It was naïve on my part to think white people don't have invisible walls. It's similarly naïve for any of us to think that rich people don't have invisible walls. We usually have no way of knowing what the next person is dealing with, what shame or guilt might be tormenting them. In Genesis, when Joseph is visited in Egypt by his brothers who are hoping to buy grain from him, we come face-to-face with the pain of the tormentor. Because of his brilliant interpretation of Pharaoh's dream, that there would be seven years of feast and seven years of famine, Pharaoh has installed him in the position of governor of Egypt. He had been sold by his brothers into slavery, but now he has risen to this elevated position of prince, riding the chariot right behind the king. He has moved on from his early hatred of his jealous brothers for what they did to him and has decided to forgive them. When they come seeking grain, Joseph recognizes his brothers right away, but they don't recognize him. He hears them talking in their Hebrew tongue and doesn't let on that he understands them. But what they are saying reveals their guilt and torment about what they did to Joseph many years before. They have suffered, just as Joseph has. What a powerful life lesson that offers to us all: no one escapes.

The dude walking around the hood with his pants sagging, wearing an angry scowl, is really not that different from the guy sitting in the C-suite. They are both tormented by invisible fences—and their torment often dictates their decision-making. One might join a gang and commit petty crimes; the other might drink himself to sleep at night or bury his pain in illicit affairs. As I travel the world, preaching in pulpits across the globe, to just as many white people as Black people, the thing that has startled me most is the realization that everybody's got a story. We all have our stuff.

When we become comfortable with disruption and have settled on the other side of the fence, at some point we come upon a discovery: we're not done yet. We keep encountering new fences we must jump. That's because life keeps changing. When I read Nelson Mandela's 1995 autobiography *Long Walk to Freedom*, I was inspired when I came across a powerful passage on the final page of the book: "So I spent my life to climb to the top of the hill, a bit winded and tired. I sat down exasperated and a bit in shock, because I spent my life to climb this mountain to get to the top, only to find out that there are more mountains to climb. So I think I'll sit here and rest a while."

That's life. When we jump the fence and get to a point of mastery, we discover there are more fences to jump. For some of us, that's an alarming discovery—so terrifying we don't want to jump anymore; we're content to stay where we are. Others will keep jumping. David was so shrewd of a fighter that he killed the lion who held the lamb in his mouth without hurting the lamb. And his reward for getting the lamb out of the jaws of the lion? A looming bear. So David killed the bear. And his reward for killing the bear was the right to fight the lion.

The prize for winning the fight is the right to enter into the next fight. All of David's life was a succession of battles that were trophies leading to him being king. And so it is with our lives: we have to learn to flourish in disruption, amid the fight.

I had a revelation when I realized the real prize of life is not the comfort that may come with riches; the real prize is the fight it takes to get there. When we decide to value the fight, we've already won the battle. We have to learn to savor that leap across the fence. That's what the gladiator feels when he goes out to fight—that spark of dopamine coursing through his body as he gears up for another battle. That's why prizefighters who have retired often climb back into the ring, because they're never happier than when they are fighting. For me, the fight is like a drug, one of the best feelings I've known. It's the gas that makes my engine roar.

The epitome of disruptive thinking is relishing the race, not the trophy at the end. Enjoying the sensation of your lungs feeling like they're about to explode, the joy of the ribbon brushing your chest as you hit the finish line. The medal they hand you is sweet, but it's really just something to stash away in a drawer or to collect dust on a shelf.

When I realized I am a gladiator, I couldn't help but to think back on my childhood years, when I could feel the sting of my father's disappointment that I wasn't going to be an athlete. I now know that I might not be able to throw a spiral, but I'm everything my father was—just on a different playing field. That was a profound revelation for me.

SEVEN

MAJOR OBSTACLES ON THE WAY TO DISRUPTION

E go.

It's a tiny little word with humongous power. In our society, we assign so many misbehaviors and misdeeds to the all-powerful ego that we might be excused for thinking we're not actually in control of our actions—we're all just slaves to our egos. The social psychologist Elliot Aronson argues that our ego is always at work trying to maintain a consistent, justifiable place in the world. It is laboring to justify everything we do, to prove that we have a role here, that we belong.

In their book, *Mistakes Were Made (But Not by Me): Why We Justify Foolish Beliefs, Bad Decisions, and Hurtful Acts*, Aronson and Carol Tavris examine how our brains are wired for self-justification. The authors look at all the work our brains must put in when we make a mistake, creating fictions that free us of responsibility so we can continue to see ourselves as smart, moral, and right.

When we leap over the fence, we're going to be making a big ask of our egos: we're going to need to be okay with being small again. We have maximized all that we could in the space we're in—we've learned and performed and found some success. We have a place there. Maybe we have become a big dog in a small kennel, the star of the off-Broadway show. Now we believe we're ready to hit Broadway. We're a bit scared, but we're poised to take the leap.

However, there are a few things we need to consider as we're about to land on that fresh new grass. The first is that we need to come as a student, not as a teacher. That means we must pull back from our previous state and do some observation and introspection. Don't be marching in there giving orders before you even know how the coffee machine works. The assignments may not be as glamorous and interesting at first, because you won't be starting out at the top rung of the ladder. The problem with getting to ten is that once you're there, you feel there's nowhere else to go. Except for eleven. And eleven is equivalent to one all over again. It's bigger than ten, but smaller than twenty.

When we jump from a job to entrepreneurship, it may take several years before we're really profitable. Along the way to profit, we have to be small again—make mistakes again, be a learner. Eventually, we hope to make it to the top in the bigger room. But that journey won't be easy. Many people choose to stay back in the old familiar space rather than risk the leap. They don't want to be small again; they don't believe their egos are up to the task.

My advice to entrepreneurs who are entering new arenas is that you need to understand that you must surround yourself with people who are smarter in the space than you are, without becoming intimidated. You can learn your way up to leading, but you can't lead if you can't listen. You must go through the listening stage, then the learning stage, and finally the leading stage.

I heard a great gentleman as he received a prestigious award drop these pearls of wisdom: Always walk into rooms where people's eyes light up when they see you. The fastest way to get any place is slowly. The top of the mountain is the beginning of the next.

If we approach each mountain with the knowledge that once we get to the top there will be another mountain, we can gird ourselves for the challenges that will come—and our egos will be nimble and resilient enough to risk setbacks. The alternative to scaling up is stagnation—becoming a monument and not a movement. Then you'll reach the end of your life and be tortured as you ask yourself, *What if I had leaped?*

As they leap, disrupters also must be prepared for criticism, attack, and condemnation—especially in a society where we often seem to be more interested in canceling than in understanding. Criticism isn't a crisis. Sometimes criticism can be constructive. If it's not—if it's destructive—we must have the discipline and focus to ignore it. How do we know the difference between the two? For one, we can ask a simple question: Is it true? Is there any element of truth in the criticism? If the person doesn't know what they're talking about, if they're misrepresenting you and don't even know you, you can't let their opinion become your reality. You have to be strong enough to walk away and keep your eyes on the goal—rather than getting distracted by the mediocre task of changing someone's mind that you may never even meet. Especially in this age of social media obsession and Twitter bullies, too many of us acquiesce to the futile effort to convince someone who is irrelevant to where we're trying to go. We want everybody to love us, so we focus on the eight people who spewed negativity at us, rather than the thousands who expressed support.

I don't care what you do; not everybody is going to love you. No matter what you say on social media, somebody's going to dispute it. You either argue back with everybody or you move on. Even in the rare instance where you succeed in the argument, what's the reward? A glimmer of satisfaction that lasts a couple of minutes, at the most? It's simply not worth the trouble.

Another important consideration is the question of energy. The energy in the next room is not the same as the energy in the room we left. We have to figure out the new pace. It may require speeding up, or maybe slowing down. There may be more hours, more meetings, more schmoozing, more delays, more examination. Or everything may come at you in a whirlwind of activity. You might have the education, but do you have the energy to move at the pace of what's across the fence?

One of the hardest lessons I've learned about hiring people is to try to discern not whether the person is able to do the job, but whether they are able to keep up with the pace in my organizations. We move at an extremely demanding pace—and that pace can't be altered because we hired you. We need people who have the energy to keep up and the flexibility to adapt to the rhythm of the room.

I know that new hires are not going to get it right away; we need to have some patience with them as they figure things out. But how much time do we give them before we decide they're not up to the task? That's a tricky question. I know that my tendency is to be too patient. One of my greatest weaknesses as a leader is that my pastor head can get in the way of my CEO head; I'll give people too much time. A common saying among CEOs is "Be slow to hire and quick to fire." But I've always had trouble living up to that because I keep holding out the hope that I might be able to help you reach the pace we require. Some people will never be able to do it; you keep waiting and waiting. Next thing you know, you've made them into a project. That's a big no-no. We don't have time to coddle employees and make them into projects. That's not what's going on here. Maybe some other type of company can afford that, but we can't. I think a few months is a reasonable amount of time to be able to see if they can keep up—as long as they're exhibiting progress and showing that they have the energy. Their energy may need to be guided and directed to make sure it's being properly allocated. They may need mentoring to understand how to apply their energy to be as efficient as possible in this new arena.

Sometimes we're disappointed in people we've hired, but we haven't effectively communicated to them the metrics by which they will be judged. We bring them in as a graphic designer and show them their desk—but fail to tell them they have to turn in a certain amount of work every day. As a leader I've been frustrated with people over things I hadn't clearly communicated; they didn't know what my expectations were. The onus in that moment rested on me to grow, when I thought they needed to grow. I need to develop a better aptitude to articulate my expectations before I have the right to be frustrated. That was something it took me a while to learn. Yes, the employee has some responsibility to figure out the pace and the energy required, but they shouldn't have to look into a crystal ball to understand what's expected of them.

If you're a chef, your pace will be different in a five-star restaurant, a home, or a buffet restaurant. At the smorgasbord, they're not asking you to decorate plates and make them pretty—they just need you to keep hot food on the line. Quantity over quality. Before you take that job, you better be aware of the difference. And the person hiring you better be keen on figuring out if you have the energy for the new job. That can be challenging, because everybody is selling themselves in the interview. Yes, I can write a script for the movie—I took several screenwriting classes and I made straight A's. But they probably didn't teach you in school that the script requires the director to be able to shoot the scenes within a certain number of days—that controls the budget for the film and determines whether it can attract the financing to be made. So, you have to write the script while thinking like a director. How many times do we have to change locations to shoot this? That's quite different from the novelist who hits the Return button and moves the action in the next paragraph from Cleveland to Paris. Screenplays don't have that luxury—that Return button might have just cost $5 million. When you jump the fence, you have to understand the expectations.

Every assignment has different nuances, whether you're an engineer or an activist, a doctor or a waitress. The title might say "lawyer," but lawyers have so many different areas of specialty. Too many dudes I know will get their lawyer from the barbershop, never verifying whether his specialty matches what they need. Are you in the middle of a beef with the IRS? Don't get a real estate lawyer. That's like hiring an oncologist to do back surgery. Don't be so enamored of the title that you don't check the credentials.

I encounter a lot of Christians who brag to me that the important people in their lives are Christians. Oh, your doctor is a Christian? That's great, but can he operate? I would rather have somebody who could operate well rather than somebody who prayed like a saint but couldn't operate. The two things aren't really congruent with each other. Oh, you married a Christian? Wonderful. But does he have a job? Does he have emotional intelligence? Is he compatible with you physically? I'm not saying the box of faith shouldn't be checked—but there are many other boxes that need to be checked as well for you to be equally yoked.

When you jump the fence, you also will need somebody to serve as a mentor, which is different from having somebody whose behavior you are modeling—which is important as well. Mentors are much more actively involved with you, cajoling, advising, cautioning, teaching you the topography of the landscape.

In addition, you also need a sponsor, somebody who will bring you into the room. Back in the old days, we called them letters of introduction—a stamp of approval from someone whose opinion matters. John the Baptist brought Jesus into the room. John had the ultimate platform, while Jesus was in the back of the room: "Behold, the Lamb of God, which taketh away the sin of the world!" (John 1:29).

He sponsored Jesus by pointing Him out and directing attention to Him. We may be great, but very often if we don't have anybody who sponsors us and authenticates the validity of what we have to contribute, we are stuck in the air and won't land on the other side of the fence the way we should. That's a prime reason why we need always to work as if someone is watching us—because we never know who actually *is* watching us. I find it interesting that when you get to know someone who might be a person of influence and affluence, they're always interviewing you just a little bit. In the back of their mind is the question that most of us at some point are thinking, whether it be in an interview or on a date: *What do I get when I get you?*

Many of us have never thought through the answer to such a question about ourselves. Do we know ourselves well enough to provide a meaningful response? Is it talent? Loyalty? Curiosity? Consistency? That brings us back to the question of our core that we discussed in chapter 4—you need to know yourself well enough to be able to explain the answer to that question. *Who are you?* The answer can go far in helping us figure out whether we will be able to bring our ego in check, whether we can adjust our energy to our new environment—or whether we will try to adjust the whole environment to fit our energy. Can we increase our efficiency without expending more effort? That one is crucial because efficiency and effort don't always correlate. For example, a track athlete can work with a coach to make their stride more efficient, thus expending less energy and requiring less effort, and still wind up running faster. Efficiency may mean less effort but more effect. Are you working as efficiently as you can, or are you expending unnecessary energy?

As I have said before, discomfort is going to come with the territory when we're being disruptive. We shouldn't even consider jumping over that fence without knowing we will experience it because we're not likely to avoid it. But we can't let the idea of being uncomfortable scare us into running in the other direction.

First of all, the discomfort is likely to be temporary. We shouldn't make permanent decisions because of temporary discomfort. Give it some time. The discomfort of growth will eventually become your norm; it will be institutionalized as part of your everyday world. And soon enough, it will be time to leap again, because you will have come upon a new fence. When Honey came upon the invisible electronic fence at one end of the property, she was still willing to brave the pain and jump again when she encountered the fence the next day at another location.

There is no greater example of discomfort becoming institutionalized than marriage. Many of the things that bothered us in the early days of our marriages don't even raise an eyebrow after we've been in it for a while. He leaves his socks lying around too much? That heat you feel on the back of your neck in the first couple of years when you spot a sock eventually becomes a shrug. You might even pick them up yourself and put them in the hamper—or you might just kick them into the corner and not add them to the wash. She leaves her shoes in an intimidating pile right at the front of the closet you share? By year five you just step over the pile and keep it moving.

The great theologian Reinhold Niebuhr had some thoughts about this in 1933. I bet you've heard them before:

> *God, grant me the serenity to accept the things*
> *I cannot change,*

courage to change the things I can,
and wisdom to know the difference.

The Serenity Prayer has been blessing us for a long time. And it's just as relevant and powerful now as the day it was written. We must come to a place of acceptance, no matter how wrenching the trauma might feel at the time. When we lose someone dear to us, after the screaming and crying and declarations that we can't go on and that God is unfair, we wake up the next day and face a harsh fact: Mama is still gone. We have to accept that and maybe enjoy the memories Mama left us with.

As I get older, my focus is leaving my children with great memories. It's not about money or *stuff*. It's about joyful days and nights overflowing with love and laughs. Those are the real treasures of life. In marriage, what makes something erotic is memory, smell, scent, touch. Little things like the way you lay your head on my shoulder, the twinkle of your eyes when you smile, the softness of your hand when I envelop it inside of mine. It's the infectiousness of your smile during the presentation you made at the corporate office, the ebullience of your greeting when you extend your hand and say, "Hi, James, how are you today?"

The challenge is being able to discern the difference between the time for patience and the time to cut your losses and step away. We can't stick around in discomfort when the situation is untenable. If you're being hurt or emotionally tormented, or your business is losing too much money, or the job is causing you trauma, you need to get out of there. You don't keep an employee who absolutely doesn't have it. There's no point in continuing to try to raise Lazarus from the dead. But only you can determine when the time is nigh to go in another direction.

We tend to extend more effort when we feel that we have a stake in the result. Of course, not every employee is going to care as much about our company as we do, but we can expect every employee to care about their own performance. When we buy real estate, we should be more eager to buy a house that was built specifically for the previous owner to live in, rather than a house constructed by a builder who cuts corners looking to maximize profits. The first house is likely to be made with higher-quality materials and greater attention to detail—that owner has a stake.

When dealing with those around me, I sometimes get frustrated by the imprecision of language. I do drills with my staff that might look to an outsider like an MC hyping a crowd at the club.

"When I say *excellent*, you say *excellent*!" I call out.

"Excellent!" I say.

"Excellent!" they respond.

Five or six times we'll go through the call and response.

There's one problem: When they say *excellent*, do they mean what I mean when I say *excellent*? My definition of *excellent* has changed about twenty times over the years. What I thought was excellence thirty years ago doesn't even compare to what I think is excellence now. With exposure and life experience, we constantly readjust, alter, transform. Do we mean the same thing when we both say *loyal*? Do we mean the same thing when we say *trustworthy*?

To clear away misunderstandings, I often will ask, "What do you mean by that?" My wife gets that one a lot. I feel the need to dig a little deeper, to check whether we are operating with different definitions. If we're working together, is your *outstanding* the same as my *outstanding*? Are we going by mine or yours? If we don't have agreement on that, we might have different outcomes. That kind of confusion is even more common if you're leaping from one arena to another—such as going from academia into business, or the pulpit to politics. You're jumping into boiling water, and you might not even realize it. A political speech isn't going to garner the same response as your Sunday sermon, where the amens come easily. An article isn't going to be written about your Sunday sermon. There won't be an opposing ad coming out distorting half of a sentence from your Sunday sermon.

While criticism is to be expected when you are a disrupter, and you can't let that stop you, I don't mean to imply that the criticism won't hurt. Being attacked, having your name dragged and dirtied, is always going to hurt. When Honey jumped the fence, I'm sure it hurt. We can't really build up an immunity that'll make the pain disappear. It hurts our children; it hurts our mother; it hurts our friends. Yes, it absolutely hurts. But what we must decide is whether our purpose is more important than our pain. The answer that we get back will go far in determining how we will function in disruption when we take the leap.

The very first thing that the book of Genesis teaches us about God is that He functions in disruption: "In the beginning God created the heaven and the earth. And the earth was without form, and void; and darkness was upon the face of the deep. And the Spirit of God moved upon the face of the waters. And God said, Let there be light: and there was light.

And God saw the light, that it was good: and God divided the light from the darkness" (Genesis 1:1–4). He functions in the midst of dysfunction.

If you're afraid of dysfunction, then don't open a business. Don't get married. Don't raise children. You have to expect that the going will get rough. It's not like people were coming by Noah's house and saying, "Hey man, let me grab a hammer and help you build this thing." That's not how this works. It's not like people were helping Moses' mother build the papyrus basket to float him down the Nile.

Everybody we read about, study, quote, and revere figured out a way to function in disruption. The people who stayed in nice, neat little cubicles? We don't make movies about them.

If the disrupter doesn't sound like your personality, if that doesn't match your demeanor, that's okay. But I bet you're only five steps removed from somebody who is a disrupter—so you need to understand how and why a disrupter moves. There's a role for you.

When my son came home from Howard University, he was supposed to work for me for the summer. There was a little bit of tension because no matter how hard he tried to see me as the bishop, as the CEO, I still was just Daddy. He had to come to a new understanding of how to interact with me. He was assigned to update my social media, so he made a lot of changes and showed them to me. But I didn't like what he had done. He had revamped the whole page.

"I don't like that," I told him.

Then he whipped out a data report and showed me how much more impact he was getting than what we were getting before.

I looked at the report, and I said, *"Ohhh."*

I was impressed. He won me over.

"So *that's* how you win an argument with you!" he exclaimed.

For me, the facts will trump all the feelings in the world. If you can show me that you have changed the bottom line, you've got my attention. For him, it was an awakening to understand how to function in my environment. From that moment on, whenever he comes to me with an idea or a change, he leads with the data.

Finding your place in a disruptive world doesn't necessarily mean that you have to be a disrupter yourself. But if you're not wired to be disruptive, how can you support the disruptions you agree with, that you think are progressive? How can you make yourself essential to the process of disruption?

EIGHT

THE CHALLENGE OF SUCCEEDING

D avid L. Steward was such a successful sales executive for Federal Express that he was inducted into the company's hall of fame in 1981—an impressive accomplishment for a Black man who grew up in the segregated South watching his father work as a mechanic, janitor, and trash collector to feed Dave and his seven siblings. Impressive, yes. But Steward wanted more. He wanted to be his own boss. So, he left his comfortable perch at FedEx to start his own company—a move that was the epitome of disruptive thinking. In 1990, he founded World Wide Technology—an ambitious name considering he had just a handful of employees in a four-thousand-square-foot office in Missouri. The idea was even more disruptive because Steward did not have a tech background.

Steward's path forward wasn't easy. There were times when he had to go without a paycheck. He once looked on helplessly as his car got repossessed from his office parking lot. But my gosh, it sure was worth every bit of discomfort. Steward's company now employs over nine thousand people around the globe and generates more than $14.5 billion in annual revenue. In 2021, Steward was the fifth richest Black man on the planet, with a net worth *Forbes* put at $5.8 billion. He is one of fifteen Black billionaires in the world.

Steward's success is disruptive not just because of how far he has come. It is also disruptive to the tech industry, a domain where I'm certain the big dogs don't sit in many meetings and witness a six-foot-four Black man stroll into the room and take up major space at the table. From where he sat at FedEx, Steward was able to envision himself jumping into a vastly different sphere—and then he actually jumped, even if it was going to mean leaving behind comfort and security.

Overcoming fear and uncertainty and making a disruptive leap is an extremely tall order. There are so many emotions and realities that you must push through in order to jump the fence like Steward did.

First of all, it's a difficult emotional transition because you customarily don't have many relationships with people in the new space. When you meet them, you're uncomfortable because they're not your norm. Anytime you jump the fence and go outside of your comfort zone, it's psychologically challenging, experientially challenging. In education circles, it's an accepted fact that middle-class kids do better in school than poor kids. When you look at graphs comparing standardized test scores against income, the graph will always look like a diagonal line headed up, like the side of a steep mountain. Research has consistently shown that student test scores are 70 to 80 percent attributable to parent income. But this doesn't mean that well-to-do students are smarter than poor students. No, what educators understand is that middle-class kids walk into the building in kindergarten already knowing how to "do" school.

Lea Hubbard, chair of the Department of Leadership Studies at the University of San Diego, said middle-class white students come to school with "insider knowledge"—knowledge of how to pick classes, take tests, and complete homework. School is a comfortable space to them; they understand its expectations and are familiar with its social norms. Teachers pick up on that insider knowledge and reward it, while punishing the children who don't have it—causing the low-income kids to reject school, thus creating a self-fulfilling prophecy.

When people from low-income backgrounds start businesses, they similarly suffer from a lack of insider knowledge. They might know how to fry the world's tastiest chicken—chicken so good that everybody who tastes it begs them to open up a restaurant. But if they didn't grow up around business owners, if they don't have an understanding of inventory, marketing, taxes, and accounting, that business is doomed to fail. People from the hood didn't grow up sitting in rooms where those discussions were taking place. They're still not in those rooms. They're more likely to be in rooms where people are talking about other people, not about marketing plans.

"Girl, did you hear what happened to Cheryl?"

When somebody does figure out how to make it out of the neighborhood, how to run a successful business, how to thrive in corporate America, they seldom come back to drop knowledge on their former peers. And I get it—it's hard to come back. If you stay on the other side of the fence long enough, you start losing touch. Transformation has occurred.

That neighborhood is no longer your point of reference. You don't remember how to talk there, how to move there. You might think you do, but the homies probably think otherwise.

When I lived in West Virginia with my young family, I could go to the grocery store with $25 and feed my kids. If my tires were wearing down, I knew where to get retread tires. I knew the dude in the community who could fix my alternator when the car wouldn't start. In my current situation, I have no idea where to get retread tires in Dallas. When something goes wrong with my car, I'm going to the dealership. Actually, the dealership is coming to me—they'll pick up my car and leave me a loaner to drive.

How do I go back to the old neighborhood and be accepted? If it's going to happen, the first thing I have to do is prove that I am one of them. The fact that I grew up there isn't really relevant. If I speak too succinctly, if I dress a certain way, if I don't have a particular swag, I can be as Black as they are and still not be one of them. I can have my Black card burned very easily—it's a delicate possession that is constantly judged. There's a long list of unspoken observations that are made; others are assessing everything about me and determining whether I am a "legitimate" brother in their eyes. Can I code switch? Am I trying too hard to code switch? (We know what that looks like—you're still probably cringing from the last time you witnessed it.) Many of us get stuck in the middle— too successful to be accepted in the hood, but too Black to be completely accepted at the country club. Maybe you've heard the saying "I can't get a GED without understanding you, but you can get a PhD and not understand me." Those in the majority have the luxury of "willful blindness," meaning they don't have to make any efforts to integrate.

However difficult it is, we must remember that change isn't totally foreign to us. Our first introduction to change is one of the most disruptive events we all undergo in our lives: birth. The egg is fertilized by the sperm cell, and the baby grows in the matrix we call the womb. The uterus becomes the world to the baby. And then he gets put out after the third trimester, sent out into this terribly foreign space. All of a sudden, he has to figure out what his nose is for—he was getting oxygen through the umbilical cord, so he never had to breathe like this. People are touching his skin. They're washing him. It's unbearably cold. The trauma is extraordinary. But he has to adjust. He finds that he can emit noises through his mouth, so he cries to express his discomfort.

This is the first clue that we're going to keep being birthed, over and over again, out of one matrix into the next. Initially we are insulated by family. Everybody we know is in the house with us. We grow comfortable with our known world. Then one day we are sent to school, ripped away from comfort. More trauma. Who are all these kids running around? Where are they going? Why is the bell ringing? What room am I supposed to go in? We go from one traumatic experience to the next; we are forced to learn adaptability. Either we become proficient at it and grow comfortable with being uncomfortable, or we become reclusive and regress back into what is safe at the expense of what is better. The expression "running back to the womb" was created to describe those who aren't able to adapt to discomfort.

Just in the past few years we've had COVID-19 and the reversing of *Roe v. Wade*, two epically traumatic events for the nation. Everything around us is evolving, changing. Yet we must adapt while the world around us is spinning. I had an experience recently that crystallized for me how hard this is. I was invited to speak at a major conference filled with wealthy titans of industry—hundreds of people who didn't look like me. In my preparation for the speech, no one told me that the stage was going to be spinning. They brought me out like I was a gladiator in the WWE, with the crowd cheering as if I were about to jump off the top rope and deliver a reverse suplex. I ran up the steps, willing the appearance of spryness into this sixty-something body of mine. This was not church at all. Hype music was blaring, sounding like the fight scene in a Rocky movie.

As I moved toward the middle of the stage, I noticed just as I was about to step that the stage was spinning! Nobody had warned me. If I didn't time it right, you might be watching a never-ending Instagram loop of Bishop Jakes falling on his butt. I had to immediately adapt to a spinning world while my mind was swirling with thoughts about what I was going to say. Those in the crowd had paid thousands of dollars to be there; they didn't care that I wasn't expecting the stage to spin. They just want to hear me say something meaningful.

That is the perfect metaphor for the times we are in. Everything is changing around us—things we didn't think would ever change. Going to the movies is a life-and-death decision? Visiting Grandma could send her to the ICU? The road down the street disappeared under six feet of water? Your state is now making it harder to vote? American citizens breaking into the nation's Capitol, the heart of the republic, trying to hunt down our most powerful lawmakers? Ugh. Where does it end?

Our ability to be adaptive and innovative and creative is constantly being challenged and hampered. All the rules are changing—but it's unclear what the new rules are. Comfort has taken a long vacation. We can't get back in the womb.

While the floor is spinning doesn't feel like the safest time to try to leap over the fence. In this destabilizing atmosphere, why am I telling you to be disruptive when you're still dizzy from the spinning floor? Well, this is exactly when we should take the leap, when the threat and the trauma are strongest. This is the environment that we are called to grow in. After all, we were born into trauma even greater than this. Mommy pushed us out even when we didn't want to leave. We had no choice but to adapt.

For more than a hundred years, scientists accepted the finding that when rats are faced with a threat, they become paralyzed by fear and accept their fate. This is such a well-accepted theory that we created clichés to describe its prevalence. "Frozen by fear." "Cornered like a rat." But in recent years scientists have pushed back on that finding. It turns out that many rats, when faced by a threat, will dart around in a frantic search for an exit. Their response is the opposite of paralysis. In other words, rats exhibit a variety of responses to threat and trauma—just like humans. Some of them give up; others try to leap the fence to move forward, to survive.

In our lives, change is constant, inevitable, never ceasing. The trauma of birth is repeated over and over again. Personal change is inevitable, from toddler to tuition. We can't escape it. Are we adaptable, or do we cleave to stability?

When you work with a personal trainer at the gym, they might put you on a ball rather than a bench to lift weights. Suddenly you're in an unstable environment—the weights are unstable, the ball is unstable, and your body is moving and shifting to stay upright. Trainers use the ball to strengthen your core, because the only way to survive is to tighten your core. That lesson is applicable to every other area of our lives—the only way to be comfortable with being uncomfortable is to strengthen our core.

Strengthening our core means having a good sense of who we are, not just what we do. Strengthening our core is not losing our grip on who we are by trying to fit in with who they want us to be. It means having the flexibility to be in unstable situations while not losing sight of our core essence and core values, remembering who we are as an individual—whether we choose to share it or not.

When we talk about our core, we have to consider two basic questions: Why are we here? Who are we here for? Many people are confronting these questions on an almost daily basis. Women might have to be a boss on the job, then come home a few hours later and be an abounding mother to all of the children and a babe in the bedroom—and then be ready for the boardroom again the next day. The stress can be overwhelming. She wants to be the mother that her mother and her grandmother were, be the lover that her husband married, and be the businesswoman that her degree has dictated she is capable of being. And on top of it all, her hair has to be right, her makeup has to be done, and she has to be comfortable making a presentation in heels.

When she hits the house at the end of a stressful workday, she is standing in front of a man who's also struggling with questions like *Who am I now? Where am I at?* The rules are changing rapidly for men, for husbands and fathers. What does it mean when his wife is more of the breadwinner? Is he head of the household, or is she? Is he expected to do more of the cooking and parenting if he's home earlier than she is? And where can he go to find answers to these questions? Probably not to his wife, who's not sure of the rules either.

The only way to survive in this environment is to not worry about what the world says. You must define your own center and know who you are as a person—not what you got, not what you own, not what you wear, not what they demand of you. Who are you right here and now? Because if you're going to jump, if you're going to speak, if you're going to take on this assignment or evolve into this new element or bring somebody into your life, you must have a sense of who you are as you're trying to learn the new assignment. This is a moment to strengthen your core—your why. That means understanding why you're jumping in the first place and what it means to you. Is this something you really want to do—or something you're trying to do because your sister did? Or because the only way your father validates you is when you respond in certain ways? Or because Instagram is telling you that this is something you should be doing?

Sometimes we need to develop methods to find ourselves when our core is in doubt. Whether it's quiet time or meditation or prayer, we need to access a way to decompress so that we can find our way back to ourselves. How do you find you?

When my mother was in the final stages of Alzheimer's before she passed away, she kept saying to me, "I can't find me. I can't find me."

I immediately understood what she meant. We were very tight and communicated really well. Sometimes life moves so fast that you lose you as you try to become what everybody else needs. In her case, she had been so jarred and turned around by the trauma of disease that she had lost her inner core, her sense of who she was. When life is rushing at us, threatening to turn us around, we have to find our core and hold on to it as tightly as we can. Find a sanctuary to help—maybe the gym, maybe the church, maybe the yoga studio. People who know how to carve out "me time" can survive and adapt to change with the most equanimity and have energy left to take on what's next. They can anticipate the next challenge while remaining present in what's happening now, like they're playing chess. Because if you're not present as a mother, if you're not present as a father, your family will suffer—and that's time you won't get back.

The hardest thing for me is to be present in the moment. My head is so full of what's next, what needs to be done, and when to prepare for what's next. Where do I have to go? What do I need to read before I go there? What do I need to have in my head? What am I going to wear? At times it feels like the present doesn't stand a chance. The danger is that I will live my life in the tomorrow and miss today. If I miss today for tomorrow, I'm just swapping moments, I'm not gaining moments. And I'm losing essential opportunities to connect to my loved ones, to revel in the joy of family. It's a constant struggle for me. Stay present. Don't lose sight of the beauty of what you have amid your distraction over what you don't. Strengthen what remains.

In his book *How the Mighty Fall: And Why Some Companies Never Give In*, Jim Collins studied the reasons some large corporations falter and ultimately fail. He identified the first mistake as hubris—when they become overconfident and forget the true foundations of their success. They take success for granted, lose the hunger to learn, get distracted by non-core areas, and confuse their why and their what. Their hubris leads them to overstretch and jump into areas where they can't be great, blindly pursuing growth for the sake of growth, without having the right people or resources in place. In other words, they lose sight of their core.

The United States rose to be one of the richest and most powerful nations in the world because of the American people's ingenuity, fearlessness, and collective resolve to keep progressing. The transcontinental railroad, the interstate highway system, the explosion of technological innovations after Sputnik that led to the internet—we envisioned these almost inconceivable advances and came together to make them happen. Each one was a major feat of disruptive thinking. But that was then. Now our two major political parties can't even come together to offer bipartisan support for legislation to rebuild our infrastructure and stop America from literally falling apart. We have lost our way; it often feels like the American core of ingenuity, fearlessness, and collective resolve may no longer be within our reach.

I'm reminded of my personal trainer—yes, I do know my way to the gym—a great guy who is not fond of elliptical trainer machines. He says they are not very useful because the machine doesn't simulate real movement. We don't really walk the way the elliptical makes us move, so you're trying to train your body to do something it doesn't normally do. With real walking or running, you develop a rhythm that requires you to put one foot down while you're moving one foot up and forward. But your feet are doing some unnatural churning thing with the elliptical machine. That's not a walking rhythm. The question before us is like the elliptical dilemma: Are we able to develop a rhythm that is present in the moment while still stepping into what's next? Can we put one foot down while the other is moving up and forward? That adaptability, that rhythm, is what we call walking. Progressing. We might stumble and fall at first, but eventually we find our equilibrium and move forward. If we try to move forward too quickly, before we have found our equilibrium, we will fall on our face. But that's okay! Because that's how we learn how to walk. We can't be afraid of falling. Often, we will fall our way forward. Everything is not going to work. Every venture is not going to succeed. Every time we try to leap across the fence is not going to result in us landing solidly on our feet. But however we land, we must learn—even if we're learning while we pick ourselves up off the ground. It's not a loss just because we took a tumble—as long as we learn in the process. That's education; there's always a tuition to be paid.

People who achieve fame or riches learn quickly that there's a tuition they must pay. When my wife lost her mother, she told me it was hard for her to sit on the stage at our church with cameras in her face while she was grieving. Privacy is very important to recovery, but she struggled because she felt like she didn't have much of it. Being famous is like undergoing a surgery in the mall. There you are, right there in the middle of the food court, or in front of the Sephora, with everybody passing by offering their opinion on what's happening to you while you're being cut open or sleeping or passing gas or doing whatever you do in the middle of a surgery. You're no less human than anybody else, but you can't really show your human frailties and faults for fear of severe backlash or derision. You are held to a higher standard, even if there is nothing inherent about you that says you deserve a higher standard. But because you make hit songs or can throw sixty-yard touchdown passes—or can preach a pretty good sermon—you're somebody's hero. So you must pay that tuition.

It doesn't matter what you're famous for, you still have a personal life and you still have problems. You have kids and you have situations and you go through everything that everybody else does—you get sick, your family members get sick, they die, they get in trouble, they get pregnant. The whole gamut of human experience. You can sing your way into being famous, but that doesn't mean you're good at handling money. You can run the hell out of a board meeting, but that doesn't mean you're good at being a wife. You can write best-selling books, but that doesn't mean you have any clue how to be a great father. That doesn't mean you're always at your best. That doesn't mean that every time you step out the door you feel like taking selfies with people. But you still have to be prepared to handle that when you walk outside and enter the public realm, because that's part of the contract you signed, even if you weren't aware when you signed it. If you can't handle that, people will attack you. I'm not crying over here, but that's the reality that fame thrusts in your face.

I must counter the previous paragraph with this: it was hard to be broke, too. I've felt the pain of worrying about paying that utility bill. It was hard to be on food stamps. It was hard to dig ditches and put in a gas line—but I did it. Every situation has its challenges, whether you're the postman or the CEO. The only place where there are no drawbacks is when our bodies move into the next state. So, we have to calibrate risks versus rewards. Because once you're up there, once you make the leap, you can't go back. You can go from famous to infamous, but you can never go back to anonymous.

The most enjoyable trips I take are when I'm able to go to a place where nobody knows me—where people brush up against me and disregard me or nearly knock me down. I find myself giggling with pleasure, because anonymity is something I can never have again in my regular life. I can have infamy, certainly—that will always be sitting out there. But I can't stuff the fame genie back in the bottle. If that's true for someone like me with a relatively narrow amount of visibility or notoriety, God help the people who really permeate all of society. That must be beyond description. We are talking the gradual death of normalcy and the rigor mortis that sets in for the lack of obscurity. As a friend once indicated to me, every move will have pros and cons, ups and downs. He said it like this: "Every *give me* has a *gotcha*!"

Anybody who jumps across that fence standing in front of them needs to know they can't go back. It's why the Red Sea closed after Moses and the Israelites crossed on their way to the Promised Land. It wasn't just so that Pharoah could drown; it was also so they couldn't go back. So that when they got out of the desert and things got rough, they didn't have the option of changing their mind and running back. Once it closed, that was it. They had to keep going forward. And so it is with life. Once you emerge from the womb, you can't go back in there. It's like the conversation Nicodemus had with Jesus before his baptism. Jesus told him, "No one can see the kingdom of God unless they are born again." In response, Nicodemus asks: "How can someone be born when they are old? Surely they cannot enter a second time into their mother's womb to be born?" (John 3:3–4 NIV).

Jesus responded that a man must be born of water and of the Spirit to enter the kingdom of God. The first time you are born by flesh from your mother, but by baptism you will be born from the Spirit.

Look at the animal kingdom, which is always rife with lessons for us humans. If an animal is birthed in the jungle and then brought into the zoo, you can't return that animal to the jungle. To be accepted back into the herd, by its tribe, is nearly impossible. After the public instituted a letter-writing campaign to get Keiko the orca (the subject of the 1993 film *Free Willy*) released back into the wild, the whale was flown to Iceland in 1999 to be released. But Keiko, who was very young when he was captured, was ill equipped to survive in the wild. He was never accepted by a wild pod and eventually made his way to a harbor in Norway, seeking the company of humans. He never managed to make it in the wild, had a difficult time hunting, and died of pneumonia in 2002.

When the African Lion and Environmental Research Trust in Zimbabwe prepares to reintroduce lions into the wild, the organization institutes an elaborate series of steps. Lions that have grown used to human contact are released into a large enclosure where they can learn to hunt prey species. They never have human contact again. Those lions eventually form a pride and birth new cubs. Only those cubs, who have grown up together as wild lions, can be released into the jungle as a pride, which will allow them to survive without having to be accepted by other wild lions.

For humans, the cost of going forward is understanding that you can't go back. Once you leap the fence, you are forever changed—and the folks back in your old neighborhood know it. You smell different, you move different, you eat different. Once you become Elon Musk, you can't become John Smith. You can't undo it. Denzel Washington will always be Denzel Washington, no matter what happens to him. Bill Cosby can never not be Bill Cosby. Your opinion of him can change, but he can never slip onto a plane and not be noticed. He can't sit in the terminal, cross his legs, and take a little snooze while waiting on his flight without everybody taking pictures of him.

I am asking you to be bold and take that leap, but I am also counseling you on the repercussions. I want you to be fully aware of the terrain you are entering. The door opens only one way. Understand that before you take the job, before you get on TV, before you run the company. You were mentioned on blogs before—now you're in the *Wall Street Journal*. That's traumatic stuff. But you were already built for this; you faced down the trauma of birth. You may not realize it, but you have survived in much more treacherous waters—and you never ran back to the womb. You knew that hinge opens only one way. Its brilliant design doesn't allow for do-overs. You are stepping onto land that may be unfamiliar and terrifying. You may not understand the language and the rules there. But that's okay. You have been preparing for this since your mother pushed you into the world. You figured out the next steps not once but over and over again. We need you to do it again.

NINE

MANAGING OR TEACHING A DISRUPTER

ave you ever had a boss or a teacher who saw things in you that you had never seen in yourself? They somehow were able to peer deep into your being and recognize that within you lay special gifts that no one had ever identified. Can you remember the sheer gratitude and euphoria you felt, the joy of finally being seen?

That's one of the great gifts that true leaders can bestow. Whether we're a CEO, a mentor, a teacher, a parent, or a supervisor, when we can stand back and detect the talents and proclivities of the people around us, help them develop those talents, and then put them in positions where they will best shine, we can transform lives. And we likely will be revered and admired by the people we lead. As many of us know from our love relationships, we are the most attracted to people who can help us discover the better side of ourselves.

This ability to truly see those around us is especially important if we are a leader who has disruptive thinkers in our midst. Disruptive thinkers may not always be the easiest to manage or to lead because their very nature is to peer outside the box, looking for a different way. Effective leaders know that the time and energy we invest in our people may not always pay off right away. In some cases, the seeds we plant and nurture will be harvested by someone else. But that's okay—we shouldn't be doing it only for our benefit. Our investment in them is a gift that they will take with them wherever they go. We must be a bit selfless and approach leadership with an attitude of servitude, as we discussed in the previous chapter.

Great leaders are like archaeologists who dig and dig until they unearth undiscovered potential. Once discovered, they recognize that this thing they unearthed has to be cultivated and protected. Sometimes people can see talents in us that we can't see because they are standing outside of us and observing, much like a therapist does with a patient. I think it is a tragedy when people rise to positions of influence who are not interested in anything other than their careers. The ability to be an archaeologist starts with ourselves—we must be comfortable enough with ourselves to be interested in investing in the well-being of someone else. We have to remember that we didn't get to where we are by ourselves; there were likely individuals along the way who selflessly poured into us. We must be able to pour into others without demanding that the harvest come back to us. We must have a broader view of humanity—the desire to want to help others for their benefit, not ours. We have to do away with that all-too-prevalent question *What's in it for me?*

One of the most frustrating experiences a human can endure is living in an environment that has deemed us invisible.

The feeling of not being seen, heard, or understood is frustrating even to those who haven't themselves recognized what they have. They still resent you for not seeing them. Ralph Ellison wrote *The Invisible Man* about the searing pain of not being seen. It is a common experience for groups who have minority status in a society. When we feel seen, we are more likely to flourish.

Too many employer-employee relationships are viewed by both parties as merely transactional—you work forty hours, and I give you pay. You write the script, and I give you credit. You prepare the consultant report, and I pay your fee. It is an injustice to your own humanity as a boss and a disservice to the employee if all the employee got out of it was pay. There is a beautiful reciprocity between effective leaders and the people they are leading. The leader can receive enormous gratification from watching their flock grow and develop as the leader places them in the best positions.

I have learned over the years in the organizations I run that when we have the right person in the wrong place, the organization will ache like a bunion to let us know something is out of alignment. The aching problems—disputes, chaos, confusion—are not always indicators that the employee is bad; the aches may be coming because we have the employee in the wrong place. Before we come to decisive conclusions about who's bad, who's good, who's evil, who's productive, and who's unproductive, sometimes we need to back up and take a deeper look at whether they've been misallocated in the role we had in mind for them. One of the downsides of being a visionary is that we can have an expectation that doesn't always incorporate the reality of what's happening on the ground. What I expected when I hired you, what I expected when I met you, what I expected when you became my friend may not be in alignment with who you really are at your core. I have to be willing to adapt my expectations to reality. I have to be willing to watch you and see what you actually bring to the table.

Leaders start by actually seeing the person who works for them, truly seeing who they are. Then they must appreciate what they see. That means paying close attention to the things the person is drawn to. Nobody has to tell a magnet to get close to metal. When you rub a magnet across wood, there will be no reaction. But when you expose it to metal, those neutrons will activate and attraction will occur, like paramecium swimming to food. The same thing happens with people—when we are interested in something, there will be an activation, an undeniable attraction. It is the job of a leader to recognize when that is happening. Do you notice that one of your employees perks up when the conversation veers toward graphic design? They seem to have an innate interest in how things look—even though they work in operations. That's likely an indicator of some attraction occurring below the surface, which may be a signal that this person is working in the wrong department.

Everyone has some degree of leadership capacity, some area where we are in a position to lead and to teach. With that position comes a certain amount of responsibility. We have to be observant enough to see when an attraction has occurred and to feed it. If I'm not curious about you, it's hard for me to curate your knowledge, to nurture and direct it. When I am talking, do I notice that particular subjects bring out a gleam in your eye? It's like those folks who walk along the beach with the metal detector wands, looking for interesting items buried in the sand. When the wand starts making a ticking sound, it has located something that may be of interest below the surface. The effective leader or teacher has to be like that wand, always cruising along the surface, looking for something that might be buried underneath.

I recently watched one of the pastors who grew up in our church being interviewed on television. Casual observers may not recognize how difficult it is to be interviewed in such a format. You don't know the questions beforehand, so once the question is asked, you only have a few seconds—at the most—to register what was asked, think about your answer, think about the consequences of your answer, and then return fire. It's a rhythm, like a conversation. You don't get to rehearse it; you can't edit it. It's just raw, right there in the moment. If you miss that moment, it's gone forever. I was so proud because he did an amazing job. I called him right away and told him how impressed I was by his ability to think that quickly on his feet. I said I called because I wanted him to hear my voice; a text message wouldn't suffice. "My God, how you've grown!" I said to him. And he ate it up. Because it's affirming, it's validating, and it's directional. It was me telling him, *I see you. I see you.*

When we don't get this, we run the risk of becoming invisible in our own house. Invisible on our job. Invisible in our school. Invisible in our church. Invisible in our own life. Eventually invisible people will erode, deteriorate, and wander away. Or destroy in a demand to be seen. Groups that are in the majority in a society have the luxury of not seeing the minority. They believe they get all their needs met without needing anyone in the minority groups, so they tend to build walls around themselves and create cocoons. The people in need can't afford to insulate themselves because they have a need outside themselves, outside their neighborhoods and communities. They have to work; they have to eat. It is so easy to lose touch with what we don't think we need. We have to be acutely aware of when we are drifting away from a world we don't live in, a community we don't have to drive through, a person we don't have to touch. It takes effort to pull ourselves back and say, *Wait, what's going on over there?* Yes, we can hibernate like a bear, cocoon ourselves like a caterpillar, but eventually that behavior will come back and bite us. As a result of our disconnection, we might find that one day we have become ignorant of that other world. Or might become victimized in ways we never imagined. Crime is often the voice of the unseen and unheard. I once heard a metaphor about Black boys that I found chilling: if Black boys don't get the warmth they need from the village, they will burn the village down in order to be warmed by the fire.

Once we have seen and identified people, it is incumbent upon leaders to expose them to an atmosphere where they can grow. A friend of mine sent me some beautiful olive trees, but I had no idea whether olive trees could grow in Texas soil. There's nothing inherently wrong with Texas soil, but olive trees flourish in Mediterranean-like climates, such as California and Florida, with hot summers and warmer winters. I wasn't sure if Texas fit the bill. For the trees to thrive, we had to understand both the soil and the needs of the trees to make sure we had a good match.

When we move people to a new environment, we similarly have to prepare both the environment and the person to make sure we get a good match. More work is necessary than when they are placed in an environment that is more natural and comfortable to them. As we cultivate them, we need to make sure they are stimulated. After my grandson finished his first year in college studying theater, he told me he wanted to work during the summer, preferably in his area of interest. I called a friend who is president of Broadway Dallas, a nonprofit that presents Broadway theater, musicals, and concerts in North Texas, and I told him I wanted him to meet my grandson. I brought my grandson to an event he normally wouldn't go to and put him at a table he normally wouldn't sit at, so he could meet somebody he normally wouldn't meet. I'm stimulating him and putting him in an environment to flourish, in the hopes that something might take root and grow out of it. I'm pleased to report he's still working there.

When I partnered with Randall Stephenson of AT&T to provide jobs for ex-offenders from our Texas Offenders Re-entry Initiative (TORI) program, I saw how difficult it was for them to step into the AT&T offices. After growing up in the hood and spending years in prison, they had to wade into an office environment in downtown Dallas. Talk about your culture shock. It's like bringing home tropical fish and putting them in a tank without letting them acclimate to the environment—it can shock the fish and kill them. Aquarists must go through a multistep process of slowly allowing the new fish to adjust to the temperature and chemical makeup of the water in the tank before they open the bag and dump the fish in the tank water. With our TORI folks, we had to make sure AT&T understood that they needed to be flexible and make some adjustments to help our people adapt. The new TORI employees needed to know that it likely would feel forced and uncomfortable at first. But just because it feels forced and uncomfortable doesn't mean they should quit and flee back to what's easy. It takes great courage to stand our ground and remain in a situation that doesn't feel natural to us. Initial discomfort doesn't mean it's not meant for us—it just means that it's new to us. We must have the mettle to remain until the adaptation occurs. But I need to add that for some people the adaptation will never happen. They may never feel comfortable; they may never thrive. That doesn't mean they are bad people; it just means we have placed them in the wrong spot. If we aspire to a culture we won't adapt to, or that won't adapt to us, we will not be successful.

Since we are talking about disruptive thinkers, leaders need to know that in some of these scenarios the disrupter may be a change agent who is trying to push us to change the way we operate. They might walk into the building wanting to shake things up, insinuating that the way things were done before doesn't work for them, or that they have ideas about how to do it better. The leader should try to get them to back up a bit. In order to be effective, disrupters must employ a sense of diplomacy that respects the culture that predates them—but have the fortitude to offer ideas to potentially disrupt that culture. Also, the submission to understand that not every idea will be accepted, not every idea may be right for the company. Not every idea is a good idea. That requires some humility. When it comes to growth and development in organizations, there isn't just one right answer. The disrupter's idea might not work in the current market, or at that particular time of the year. Disrupters must engage in a delicate dance in organizations.

If the boss doesn't let their idea win the day, it may trigger feelings of rejection, which could prompt the disrupter to flee. Everybody has to be sensitive and aware of how quickly the relationship can sour.

When a couple is in the market for a new house, that two-story Craftsman on Cedar Lane might be lovely, but if the local schools aren't very good, it doesn't work because they have young kids. Fast-forward fifteen years, and when the kids are gone, the Craftsman might be ideal. Fast-forward another twenty years, and now the five bedrooms are unnecessary and climbing the long staircase up to the second floor fifteen times a day is a concern. Decisions have expiration dates on them. Timing is everything.

All growth is disruptive and comes with growing pains. The very nature of progress is disruptive. The goal for disrupters should be to initiate disruption without destruction, disrupting to the point that it grows while respecting the environment and not destroying the fundamental core. I can't change the weather in Texas. I can't change the soil in Texas. All I can do is plant the olive trees in a way that makes them feel most comfortable. So far, the trees are growing wonderfully. My grandson is also doing very well in the theater environment. But the story isn't over yet—the boy is still in school. The trees still haven't borne any olives. After all, that is the true test. Will it provide a harvest in the new environment? Will it be fruitful? When Jesus cursed the fig tree, the tree didn't lack leaves, roots, or branches. It lacked fruit, prompting him to render it forever fruitless. We can't exist in a fruitless life, or a fruitless job, or a fruitless marriage, because fruit is the ultimate indication that the cultivating has been successful.

In addition, we have to see it through all seasons, through hot and cold, through droughts and floods. Will it be able to withstand the wages of time and climate change?

If the environment doesn't work for the tree, perhaps it will fare better somewhere else. So, we move it again, starting all over. That is the perfect analogy for the disrupter: sometimes we have to try again in a different environment. It might take much of your lifetime to get it right. Because every time you think you got it right, it changes again. By the time you get good at eating out together as a couple, knowing exactly how long it's going to take the wife to get dressed and put on her makeup, and how many times the husband will change his tie or his shirt before he's ready, then you have a baby. That system you developed is thrown out the window because it's meaningless now. By the time you get good at remembering to pack all that baby gear in the bag—the extra clothes, the extra diapers, the baby wipes, a spare pacifier—the kid is walking and you don't need a bag anymore. You get accustomed to dining with your little one and selecting restaurants that can accommodate his weird food preferences, and then what happens? The kid is driving and has no interest in going anywhere with you. Next thing you know, they're gone and their room is empty—and you're looking across the table at a spouse you haven't seen without kids for twenty years. Now you have to remember what restaurants you both used to like—and even what regular dinner table conversation sounds like.

We're constantly experiencing disruption, change, transformation, even if we don't always realize it. Life itself is disruptive; we have to be adaptable. We might need to cover the olive tree in the winter to protect it from the cold. And when that disruptive new employee interrupts the business meeting to explain her new idea, we may need to pull her to the side to let her know that wasn't the right time and place for it. Maybe she should have done that over coffee or over lunch. However, we also may realize that the end of the business meeting is actually the ideal time for new ideas—and we have to be flexible and humble enough to admit that. Two years later, the company business meeting might proceed in a totally different fashion. Everything is always changing.

When we recently sat down to discuss releasing a new music project based on the Woman Thou Art Loosed conference, I was shocked to discover how much the music business had changed since the last time we put out a recording some years back. Before, it was all about talking to radio DJs and getting the product on the shelves. Now it's all downloads and mechanical royalties and getting used as background music on TikTok videos. A radically different business model has emerged. In the meeting, the folks who were experts in the old system were clashing with the younger folks who understand the new way. We finally compromised on an approach that combined old school and new school. And I'm pleased to say that it appears to have worked—for a while, we were number three across all platforms on iTunes and number one in Christian music. But man, did we have to go through some uncomfortable moments to get there.

When managing a disrupter, we have to put them in safe environments that allow for disruption. That gives them the freedom to toss out ideas and see what sticks and what doesn't work. At the same time, in that safe place, they learn that there is a time and a place for orthodoxy, when the old way is indeed the best way. They must submit to the protocols already in place. There is a time to shine and a time to shut the heck up. The best way to manage disrupters is to teach them. Talk to them. Guide them. Stroke them. Support them.

The entrepreneur and businessman John Hope Bryant says that Black people flourish in an environment where the floor is flat and the rules are clear. If you put us on a basketball court or a football field, where the ground is flat and the rules are clear, we become superstars. If you put us in a company where the floor is flat and the rules are clear, we excel. If the floor is flat, secretaries become CEOs. But if the floor isn't flat and the rules aren't clear, we will struggle. In many ways, this describes much of our time in the post–civil rights era, trying to figure out how to make a way in confusing and uncomfortable systems. People from minority groups will struggle to find success when trying to discern the confounding ways and rules of the majority—particularly if those rules were partly constructed to keep the minorities on the outside looking in. If the floor is tilted, by definition some people are going to be higher than others. Somebody will be starting out the one-hundred-meter sprint already ten meters ahead at the starting gun—or standing on third base, telling themselves they hit a triple. Our society has made strides in leveling the floor, but there is still much work to be done. We now install elevators and ramps in buildings so people with disabilities will have the same access as everyone else. We built rooms in the Potter's House specifically to accommodate children with autism, so the environment doesn't overstimulate them. We must be intentional about leveling up—whether we are talking about race, ethnicity, religion, gender, or disability. We must make sure all of our systems operate with flat floors and clear rules.

In many ways, the challenge schoolteachers face is figuring out a way to level up the classroom when students from a vast array of circumstances walk through the door. Some kids will have eaten a full breakfast and been driven to school, while another might have left a house without breakfast after watching their mother get beaten half to death the night before. One kid hasn't seen their mother in months and is living with an overwhelmed and destitute grandmother, while another doesn't even have a home to live in. Those kids clearly are not going to be in the same position to learn and thrive, yet that's the school system's expectation. They will be compared to one another every day and penalized if they don't perform in a way that far-off education bureaucrats have deemed they should. And, increasingly, the teachers also will be penalized if their students don't meet state standards. It's a brutal, disturbing system.

If they are able to make it to college, the kids from chaotic homes and underfunded schools will be expected to perform at the same level as kids from well-to-do homes with stable families. For those kids, the floors have never been flat and the rules continue to be unclear.

We have so many examples in our society of people who did not thrive in school because they were disruptive thinkers who had a hard time coloring inside the lines. Jay-Z. Ray Kroc. Quentin Tarantino. Walt Disney. Tom Cruise. George Carlin. Chris Rock. Richard Branson. John Travolta. Whoopi Goldberg. They all dropped out of high school but went on to find enormous success.

A teacher is charged with managing and teaching the disrupters—along with thirty other students who need individualized help. A gargantuan, nearly impossible task.

The courage to be authentic is extremely valuable. You will be roundly attacked for it—usually by people cleaving to structure and orthodoxy. Prolific filmmaker Tyler Perry broke all the rules when he started out with his stage plays and transitioned to film. But eventually he swallowed up all his critics and built one of the largest studios in the business—in Atlanta, not Hollywood.

Nobody writes about rule followers. They're not the ones who turn heads and transform systems. But if you're still afraid of leaping over that fence, just consider that the thinking we now consider orthodox used to be seen as disruptive. Imagine the eye-bulging consternation that greeted the first dude who decided to hunt for edible mushrooms that wouldn't kill you. Or the first person to conclude that it was okay to drink the milk from a cow or a goat. The new orthodoxy used to be disruptive. What is now widely accepted at some point was looked upon as heresy. This should be solace to the ears of all the disrupters out there—if you're right, they all will soon be following you.

But if you're a true disrupter, that will be your signal to find the next fence to leap over.

TEN

BEING MARRIED TO A DISRUPTER

As we lay out the challenges facing disrupters, I'm sure many of you are wondering whether you have the spirit of a disrupter. Are you built to constantly be jumping over these fences? You should know that everybody is not made to cause disruption. Some of us were put here to be a support to disrupters—and that role can be just as important as the disruption. If you're not a disrupter, it's more than likely that you are in close proximity to one. You may be married to a disrupter, or the parent of a disrupter, or the teacher or manager of a disrupter. Fence dwellers are the stabilizing force to disrupters, so their presence is vital to the disrupter being able to thrive.

Many of us wind up marrying our opposite. Like the poles of a magnet, we are often attracted to the things that we don't have, the things we are not. If you're a person who's disruptive, you marry the hands that bring you normalcy and stability. My wife, Serita, is stable, while I'm all over the place. I need her to save me from my own creativity. If I decided tomorrow that I was through with all this craziness and told her I wanted us to live on a boat in Indonesia, she'd say, "You crazy fool—let's go." But she'd make sure the boat had every possible thing we'd need to live in comfort. We all need the fence dwellers as much as the fence jumpers.

In a corporation, we can't have a workforce filled with disrupters. We need somebody maintaining stability, somebody making sure the bills get paid and the payroll is met. We need Bentley as well as Honey. Without Tonto, the Lone Ranger was just a white dude on a horse getting into scrapes he couldn't get out of. Batman without Robin wouldn't have found a way to escape the disruption he caused without somebody slashing the tires of the Batmobile. Johnny Carson needed Ed McMahon as the straight man to react to his silliness—Ed was us, laughing on our couches at home. A choir of all soloists will sound like a mess. Disrupters need hands beneath our wings, keeping us afloat.

We were struggling. The Union Carbide plant where I worked in West Virginia had shut down, and my unemployment was just about to run out. I had a small church in Montgomery, about forty minutes from our humble little house with the peeling white paint in Dunbar, West Virginia. I was in the process of trying to figure out how I was going to build myself back up. It was going to require some re-creation.

One day Serita and I were sitting on the raggedy couch in our living room watching television. The couch was so shabby that we covered it with a bedspread to hide the log underneath that was helping to keep the couch upright because one of the legs had broken off. Yeah, we had a three-legged couch. As I said, we were struggling. I looked up and felt like I was seeing our fireplace with fresh eyes. And I didn't like it. About five feet across, the area above the fireplace had a wood mantel I had painted black and faux black-and-white brick I had installed. I was not feeling the overall look any more.

"You know what?" I said to Serita. "I think we should put in a new fireplace. We can brick the entire wall and put a concrete ledge across it."

"Yeah, that would be nice," Serita said.

Well, that was enough confirmation for me. "I'll be right back," I said.

I went out and retrieved a crowbar from the trunk of my car. When I got back in the house, I walked straight to the fireplace and started ripping the mantel off the wall.

"What are you doing?!" Serita yelled.

"I told you—I'm gonna build a wall and put a new mantel up here. I have to take this down."

Serita looked at me in horror—in her eyes, I was a crazy man wielding a crowbar. But I knew if I tore it down, I would fix it. I went out and bought some bricks; I got a buddy to lay them. We put up a concrete mantel to finish the rehab. It turned out beautifully.

If she didn't know before that day, Serita realized then that she was married to a disrupter—or a man who was mentally depraved. We laugh hysterically about that memory now. It was a great predictor of the future.

Many years later, my ministry was growing, and we were living in a much nicer house that we had purchased two years earlier in an affluent neighborhood in West Virginia. We had worked like dogs to get that house. In fact, it was so nice that some people criticized us for it: *Why is Pastor living so well?* We had worked to put our stamp on the house. Finally, it felt like the house we wanted.

"Honey, I think we're leaving," I said to her one day.

"Leaving?"

"Yeah, I can hear it in my preaching. I think I'm finished here."

"And go where?" she asked.

"That building I went to see down there in Dallas—I can't shake it out of my head."

Without hesitation, Serita said, "If you're going, I'm going with you."

And I did. And she did. As the saying goes, the rest is history. When I got to Dallas, my vision was very disruptive. With two people on my staff, $8,000 in the bank, and no camera, I had my sermons aired on national television. Because we couldn't afford a camera, for the first two years we aired footage of me preaching at churches that had cameras.

When we were dating, I had told Serita, "Stick with me, and I'm taking you places you've never seen and showing you things you couldn't imagine."

I had no idea how I was going to do that. But I did. Together, Serita and I have traveled the continents of the world— guests of the president of Uganda, the king of Swaziland, the president of Zimbabwe, the president of Trinidad, and multiple presidents of the United States. And it all began in that raggedy little house with Serita's first real glimpse that I'm not afraid to tear down the wall—and build it back better.

When we think about the trials that a spouse will endure when being married to a disrupter, much of it revolves around the question of whether we can learn to accept difference. That's a foundational challenge undergirding every relationship, particularly a marriage. Difference can be terrifying. After all, we're most comfortable around people who are like us. But it also can be beautiful.

I admit that I'm a bit obsessed by difference. I often will have deeply intriguing but irrelevant questions pop into my head. *Does chocolate taste the same to your taste buds as it does to mine? Do you have an inner voice actually talking to you like I do when you ponder life's perplexing questions?*

Our brains are as unique as our fingerprints. The way we think is triggered by neurons that release chemicals in our brains, known as neurotransmitters, that generate electrical signals in neighboring neurons like a wave sweeping across our brains. The result is the formation of a thought. Our neurotransmitters are all different; our waves are different. As a result, we have different ideas on everything ranging from the colors on the wall to the spiciness of the chili. In fact, our creativity derives from our uniqueness. Lawyers and psychologists know that eyewitnesses at the scene of a crime will report seeing different things—that blue car in one report becomes green in another. Therefore, it is a futile pursuit for those of us in relationships to think we are supposed to have the same reaction to the same stimuli and experience. Humans just don't work like that.

When faced with the vagaries of human behavior, Serita will think in terms of black or white, good or bad. Everything with her is an absolute. However, I think in shades and variances. I dance in the grays of life. She focuses on what the person did—period. I tend to focus on why they did it. One day during a debate, she told me, "You could be Judas's lawyer!" We both burst out laughing.

She's not wrong for how she processes input; she's just different—and she has that right, which I must respect. It's clear to us that sharing the same address and even the same bed has not created in us homogeneity of thought. But we didn't start with such clarity. It took years for us to appreciate our individual uniqueness rather than seeing it as relationship dysfunction.

As we have worked out this marriage thing over the decades, a disrupter and his lover, I have formed some thoughts on how to keep it together:

Stop fighting to be right. It's counterproductive to judge your companion's responses, likes, and dislikes using yourself as the metric. Repeat after me: "I am not the standard." It is the epitome of arrogance to approach problem-solving by elevating one perspective over another. We know opposites attract—and then become increasingly frustrated with the other person's uniqueness. Don't fall into that trap. Most people are too gracious to say it out loud, but the customary pattern is that one imperfect person will become angry with another imperfect person for not being imperfect in the same way they are. Of course, there are boundaries for what is intolerable behavior, but the measurement can't be based on who is the most verbal, who is the more outgoing, who is the best educated. Why? Because that would be manipulation. Transactional relationships are likely to be controlled by income, sex, emotional abandonment, or whatever currency that can be used to win. However, the real triumph begins when both of you start working toward solutions and stop fighting to be right.

Your lover is not your enemy. When I counsel couples, I often get the feeling that they are two prizefighters squaring off in the ring. They've been at each other's throats so long that they can no longer even see that it is the issue that is causing the pain, not this individual you really love and cherish. When you separate the issue from the individual, you create an opportunity to join forces against the issue rather than drop bombs on each other. I realize that there will be times when it's difficult to separate the issue from the individual, especially when the individual is complicit in creating the issue. Take a deep breath and try to create a safe space for the individual to help you understand the root cause of why this particular issue is difficult for you. Resist the temptation to point out how you don't have the same issue, because when your inadequacies are the topic, you've built a point of reference that is reciprocal, tit for tat, regarding conflict resolution.

Never use the children or in-laws as a mechanism for torture just because you're hurt. This is very damaging to the children and other family members. Don't be surprised when the damage spreads. When children are used as a stick to damage spouses, it usually works. But the price of winning is a frayed, damaged child. A disappointing wife doesn't always equate to a disappointing mother, and a disappointing husband doesn't always equate to a disappointing father. If the family can grow into a consistent unit, it's way better than a lifelong rivalry.

Traditional roles don't always work with nontraditional people. Most of us got our opinions about what we want or don't want from the family culture we grew up in. When we got married, I told my wife, "I'm not marrying your family, and you're not marrying mine!" Sounds good, doesn't it? I thought so, too. But the truth is, marriage is like a corporate merger. Given thirty minutes and a hefty payroll, we can have a wedding. But turning a wedding into a marriage takes much longer. Since no gender is a monolith, we can't afford to expect stereotypical roles—especially when we have a disruptive thinker trapped in a role they don't have the skill set or temperament to navigate.

Trust is about more than fidelity. While infidelity can be as fatal as rat poison to a rodent, it's certainly not the only breach of trust that is difficult to heal. There's economic trust, emotional trust, intentional trust, and so many more. In the lists of the leading causes of divorce in the US, money is always near or at the top. Who makes what? Who spends where? Who is manipulating whom for comfort and a sense of well-being? Emotional safety is the elixir of intimacy. Until his feelings, vulnerabilities, sorrows, and secrets are safe in you, he will always remain guarded. If she confides something personal about her family and you use it against her in an argument, don't expect vulnerability to come easily again. If you know he's got abandonment issues and you keep threatening to leave, you are pulling triggers with no idea of how much damage that bullet will bring. Let's always try to make a quick assessment of actions versus intentions. I remember a mother who accidentally ran over her child backing out of a garage. She was horrified, devastated. None of her pain repaired the damage; the child was still gone. However, the courts don't just consider the actions, but also the intentions. Do you?

Understanding doesn't necessarily align with condoning. What we desperately crave in a relationship is to be understood, to have a safe place to live where we are not constantly being judged instead of understood. I don't have to be depressed to understand your depression. Empathy isn't a result of uniformity. It's the ability to understand what someone else is experiencing and to approach their trauma from their unique perspective, rather than your own. A keen example is the way in which God speaks to Abraham about asking Hagar to leave. His empathy is unrivaled, yet His will was irrevocable.

> *And Sarah saw the son of Hagar the Egyptian, which she had born unto Abraham, mocking. Wherefore she said unto Abraham, Cast out this bondwoman and her son: for the son of this bondwoman shall not be heir with my son, even with Isaac. And the thing was very grievous in Abraham's sight because of his son. And God said unto Abraham, Let it not be grievous in thy sight because of the lad, and because of thy bondwoman; in all that Sarah hath said unto thee, hearken unto her voice; for in Isaac shall thy seed be called. And also of the son of the bondwoman will I make a nation, because he is thy seed. And Abraham rose up early in the morning, and took bread, and a bottle of water, and gave it unto Hagar, putting it on her shoulder, and the child, and sent her away:*

and she departed, and wandered in the wilderness of Beersheba. (Genesis 21:9–14)

Notice how God handled Abraham with empathy. Once he felt understood, he complied. The outcome was disruptive, but not destructive. Relationships work best when empathy replaces ultimatums.

Agree to disagree. All disagreement doesn't have to lead to divorce. After more than eight years of silence, Laura Bush said in an interview with CNN's Larry King that she backs gay marriage and abortion—and that they were points of contention with her husband, former president George W. Bush. Mrs. Bush was promoting her memoir *Spoken from the Heart*, in which she writes about her life both before and after becoming first lady. In response to a question about gay marriage, she said, "There are a lot of people who have trouble coming to terms with that because they see marriage as traditionally between a man and a woman. But I also know that, you know, when couples are committed to each other and love each other, that they ought to have, I think, the same sort of rights that everyone has."

Mrs. Bush said she and her husband "disagree" on legalizing same-sex marriage. My point here isn't to sway your thinking on the subject either way. I'm just pointing out that two very different perspectives don't have to end in divorce. I fear that this art of disagreeing without being disagreeable is becoming lost in our society. The country has suffered from the death of respect and even healthy debate—no matter the issue. We see all dissenters as enemies. That can only lead us to more pain and dissolution.

Don't burn down the school. In West Virginia I once heard a man say something I will never forget: "Just because you graduated doesn't mean you can burn down the school!" His quote comes to mind when I think about what happens in my house during the holiday. From November to January, my wife transforms from Serita Jakes to Mrs. Santa Claus. Everything in my house is blinking, while Patti LaBelle, Mariah Carey, Lou Rawls, Luther Vandross, and everyone else's Christmas album is in constant rotation. The trees are lit, the fireplace is crackling, the manger is adorning the yard, and light-clad angels are draping the property. On the other hand, I'm not quite Ebenezer Scrooge, but I don't like putting up anything we have to take down in ninety days! My mind can't quite wrap around the logic of that. However, though it's not really my cup of tea, when I see how much joy it brings her, I find myself humming right along with Luther. In this case, she's the disruptive thinker. But over the years, I've come to appreciate the touches of lace she adds to my life. In other words, I'm still in school. Are there areas in your life where you are losing the main point of your coupling over issues that damage the individuals you say you love?

Serita and I have seen each other through all manner of rich and poor, sickness and health. When we were struggling, she managed a Rite Aid for a while. When my mother was dealing with Alzheimer's, we brought her into our house. Serita rushed to her mother's bedside until she passed. Whatever it took. When 9/11 happened, I was in another part of the world, far away from her and my family. I didn't know what was going to happen next, but I knew I had to get home. Even though the airways were shut down, I got special permission to ride on a baggage flight. I flew strapped to a jump seat to get to my family. Whatever was happening to us, I wanted to fight it from home surrounded by people I loved.

My wife is so emotionally honest, I have had to learn to accept it without trying to change it. That all bubbled to the surface when we visited the White House and she met Michelle Obama. She's always been fascinated with first ladies and even had a relationship with Laura Bush, but her feelings about the beautiful, brilliant Mrs. Obama are on a whole other level. In addition to her awe of the first lady's overall grandeur, Serita sees Michelle's relationship with her mother as a reflection of the relationship she had with her own mother.

There we were in the Oval Office, meeting the first Black first couple, trying to be cool and dignified. But when we saw Michelle, I felt a rush of anxiety, because I know my wife. I was thinking, *Don't lose it. Don't lose it.* Right on cue, Serita burst into tears. Mind you, not a little tear rolling down the cheek, but full-on bawling. She was completely overwhelmed by the moment. I couldn't believe it; she was having a meltdown in the Oval Office in front of the president and first lady. I wanted to kill her right there on the spot for embarrassing me. I was sure the Secret Service was going to rush in and drag us out. When Michelle reciprocated the love, I breathed a sigh of relief. In retrospect, the scene was hilarious. That's my wife—never one to hold back. And I love her for that.

To all my friends who are married to disrupters: let there be peace on earth, and let it begin with you!

ELEVEN

PARENTING A DISRUPTER

Years ago, I heard a story about a woman who learned how to bake a ham from her mother. Growing up, she would watch closely as her mother carefully cut off the butt of the ham, place the ham in the pan, soak it in apple juice, coat it with brown sugar, and decorate it with pineapples and other garnishes before she placed it in the oven to bake. The woman was impressed by how much care and love her mother put into the whole process. When she grew into an adult, on special occasions she would follow her mother's ham baking recipe like scripture, making sure she matched every step—including the love she put into it.

One day when her mother was visiting, the woman prepared the ham just as her mother always had, carefully following each step. After the woman placed the ham in the oven, her mother looked at her with a frown.

"Why do you cut off the butt of the ham?" the mother asked.

The daughter smiled. "Well, because I watched you growing up. You always cut the butt off the ham. So I do, too."

Her mother responded, "I cut off the butt because my pan was too small."

Far too many of us learn to live within the restrictions of the previous generation without even realizing that the restrictions are not reflective of our realities. When we become parents, we run the risk of raising our children within the parameters we were raised in—and then we chastise our children for not following rules that are no longer relevant. We are cutting off their butts to fit into pans that have long since been discarded, stashed in the back of the pantry, or given away to Goodwill.

The great thing about every new generation is that they are predisposed to test the boundaries. That's what young people do—they push past the guardrails and try to set their own course. In other words, they feed off disruption, looking for new and hopefully better ways. Because we have a fidelity to a system that fit our era, sometimes we misunderstand their disruption as rebellion, not recognizing that time has made our old parameters almost irrelevant. Children are taught by previous generations—whether by parents or teachers—who have a dogma and a creed that is built around their experiences, which are often not applicable to the situations the children find themselves in today. Young people step on a college campus with their parents' words ringing in their ears about how they need to find a stable career like accounting or law—only to discover that the term *stable career* may not even be relevant anymore in an era when they might change careers half a dozen times before they hit forty.

Before I go further, let me say that I am not a trained psychologist or psychiatrist. My views on parenting come from three streams of experiences.

First, in my four decades as a pastor, ministering to more than thirty thousand members, not only have I gained the benefit of my own experiences, but I have had the pleasure of interacting with other people, other families, other children. That's an unbelievable focus group that provides a unique lens to see how problems arise in families. When families are in crisis, they generally come to their pastor. You see people at their best and also their worst. In forty-six years of dealing with families who had children that were classified as "troubled," I've seen that in many cases they were just children whose butts were cut off to fit a pan that no longer applied. Are we cutting off the potential greatness of our children because of our loyalty to a past that no longer exists?

Second, I am a parent to five children and a grandparent to nine. Time has given me a multigenerational perspective. I have watched what time does to truth, how it disrupts and warps parenting orthodoxies and conventions. Our methods have to adjust in order to remain relevant to our children, or we will punish them for our inflexibility rather than enhance their creativity.

Third, my own journey growing up in a world that doesn't always seem to grasp the power of difference and doesn't understand that the brain is as unique as a fingerprint has shown me that we all think and act differently. That's why there are so many different peach cobbler recipes, or ways to make banana pudding, or methods to build a car. There isn't any one right answer for every child, because every child is unique. Some children are on the autism spectrum, some are slow learners, some are geniuses, some learn better through visual aids rather than reading materials. Every child is a mystery that every parent has to handle uniquely. None of my five children are alike—all have different personalities and different methods of learning and different paths to come to a conclusion.

Many years ago, I had the privilege to go to Nairobi, Kenya, which I have since visited quite a few times. I went to dig boreholes for people who had no water. Eventually I adopted a hospital that we would raise money and resources to help. When I went to visit a school, I was struck by the deficit of books in the library. I told the head of the school that when I got back home, I would gather up books in Dallas and send them back to her in Kenya. But she stopped me right there.

"We can't use American books in our school," she said, "because our method of teaching is similar to that of Great Britain. The method of teaching we use is based on memorization, and on learning the answer. Whereas the teaching mechanisms that are used in America don't necessarily provide the answer. They present the question and teach you to think toward the answer."

Because we have a system that doesn't make us memorize a particular answer, we have the freedom to think creatively, to step outside the parameters. We have to honor that inclination in our children, rather than try to stifle it when it makes us feel uncomfortable or threatened. The struggle with raising disruptive children is that it is often easier to think that there's something wrong with the child than to challenge the limitations of the system. Some children may seem to be troublemakers because their pan is too small. John Lewis, Martin Luther King Jr., Fanny Lou Hamer—all were young people who were thought to be rebellious by their own parents. They did not fit within the pan as their parents saw it—be quiet, make the best of the situation, sit down on the bus and be silent, go where they tell you to go. And then this forty-two-year-old Black woman, Rosa Parks, decided she would sit where you're not supposed to sit. Was she wrong—or was the pan wrong?

When we look at each child, we must be open to the possibility that maybe the parameters need to be changed rather than the child. I understand that this approach at times may feel scary and potentially dangerous for people who have spent significant time in oppression. After all, refusing to stay inside the parameters could cost you your life; venturing outside of them can be terrifying.

But this doesn't just apply to racial oppression. Your family, no matter your race or creed, can be the source of your feelings of oppression. You might have five doctors in your family and be expected to follow the family tradition—but you want to be a writer. These truths are self-evident among the wealthy as well as the impoverished. It's just a different set of expectations—but expectations that can be crippling to creativity. They may see your creativity as dysfunction rather than disruption, just because you didn't live up to what they had in mind. We can never predict how that sort of rejection of the child will manifest in the child's life. Will it cause insecurities and self-doubt? Will the child conclude that their creative impulses, or their desires to break away from family tradition, are wrong? I live in a family of scientists, and I want to be a guitarist—am I wrong? I live in a family of musicians, and I want to be a scientist—am I wrong? I see these family dynamics play out all the time—parents trying to cram the child into a world that's more the parents' than the child's.

It happens quite often with faith. Preacher's kids forced into the ministry, miserable all the while, because they come from three generations of preachers.

Instead of asking our children "How are you?" maybe we need to place a greater emphasis on the question "Who are you?" That means we have to go from just teaching to listening. If we listen to them, we will be better able to put them in an environment where they will flourish. I've had many beautiful plants that died because I put them in the wrong environment to thrive. More sunlight or less? Is the soil too rich? The last one thrived with oodles of sunlight—why is this one reacting differently? Our children are all different, and each might require different soil, or more sunlight. We won't be able to figure that out if we're not listening to them. Add to that the tendency, as I mentioned earlier, to be a more effective parent when raising the child who is most like us. The ones who aren't? We just don't understand why they won't act right. We're an extrovert, wondering why the kid is so quiet. "Lisa, what's wrong with you?" Which is just another way of saying *Why can't you be more like me?* And in an instant, we've created trauma in the child's life when the child just wanted to be herself, not us. This is a racial truth—you're not Black enough. A family truth—you're not pretty enough. A sibling truth—you're not like your brother.

From a child's perspective, history can be its own form of oppression. History dictates so much of what the child will face: how it was done before; how it was done with me when I was your age; how it was done when we lived down South. Parents may see history as providing them with wisdom, which it often does. But from the child's view, that historical wisdom might look a whole lot like oppression.

Every creative person disrupted something to be creative. We never write in our history books about people who fit in; we only write about people who stand out. Yet we train our children to fit in while they read about people who stand out.

As I said before, my father was a tremendous athlete. He was such a skilled football player that he was pursued by the NFL's Cleveland Browns. In the Mississippi schools where he played, there are still pictures of him on the wall. When I was growing up, my brother was also really good at sports. I was seven years younger than my brother, so I would sit and watch them play in the yard—knowing that I did not fit on their playing field. I grappled with my suspicion that something was wrong with me because my interests were so different from theirs. The great liberation of my life occurred when I reached a place where I gave myself permission to be me. No longer did I entertain the idea that I was inferior because I was different. It was okay that I had no interest in sports, because I was good at other things. (Though I admit that my aversion to sports can still cause me some discomfort. If I'm among a group of men talking about football, I'll feel a little uneasy, wondering whether I should be able to join the conversation. It never totally goes away.)

If you have been told that your child is disruptive and causing trouble in school, you should be paying close attention to what's actually going on with the child. It's important to find the soil in which that child flourishes. That becomes a process of trial and error—you might have to get them into several activities before you find the one that works for them.

Among my children, the one who is now most famous is the child who gave us the most trouble and broke all the rules. Sarah has told her story many times in her ministry, sermons, and *New York Times* best-selling books—how she became pregnant at thirteen and was shunned at school and gossiped about at church, but eventually found her way back to God. Her story is the foundation of her incredibly successful mega-conference, Woman Evolve. At the end of the thirtieth and final Woman Thou Art Loosed (WTAL) conference in September 2022, I officially passed the torch to Sarah and her Woman Evolve conference. It was a powerfully emotional moment for me, for Sarah, for our family, and for the thousands watching in the audience and millions who viewed it at home.

"This is not an inheritance; this is a calling," I told Sarah when she joined me on the stage. "I respect God too much to throw somebody up here just because they're kin to me."

We played the video of the night when Sarah introduced me at a WTAL conference many years ago, when she was still a girl. That was when her journey to the summit began. She told the story that night of how she was liberated when I welcomed her and her son Malachi back to the church after he was born. She knew then that I had her back. She has shown incredible courage over the years as she ascended from that moment, walking through the judgment, the hate, and the doubt, and becoming a powerfully influential pastor and leader of women and men.

As I handed her the torch at WTAL, I told the story of how when she was a girl and told me from the back seat of the car that she was cold, I would pull the car over and wrap my coat around her because I loved her. So, I took off my jacket onstage in September and draped it over her, to show that I would always be there to warm her, protect her, love her. There wasn't a dry eye in the house.

This kind of parenting is expensive. You put all your chips on the table with the prayer that it will work, but you're not really sure that it will work. Sarah has an anointing that causes people to want to hear her. But she was mighty disruptive growing up. A unique force of nature. I can hear her uniqueness in the way she addresses a text, in the way she processes the truth. What we want to do is allow our children to be authentic, not duplicative.

When we are faced with a disruptive child, before we bring in the heavy artillery of psychiatrists and psychologists and drugs like Ritalin, before we make the child feel like they have a sickness, we must make sure the problems can't be resolved by more focused parenting. We live in a world where we want to respond to every "problem" with a quick fix. An estimated one out of every thirteen children in the US takes some sort of psychiatric medication.[1] But with parenting, you don't fix anything quickly. The fastest way to get there is slowly. Of course, there are some children who need medical assistance to cause their brains to function effectively. But pills have become a catch-all solution for busy people to resolve every child's problems. In the US, we medicate our children far more than any other country. In many cases, there may be other factors at work, other reasons they are acting up that don't require drugs to fix.

Sometimes, a child causing disruption is a symptom of disruption in the family. The turmoil in the child is akin to holding a mirror up to the family itself. Recently I was working with a family in which there had been molestation and divorce.

The eight-year-old boy had been acting out—tearing up walls, jumping out of windows, kicking over chairs, talking back to teachers. At first, I thought he missed the firm hand of a father speaking into his life, so I was kind of tough on him. But the second time I saw him, I decided to try a different approach. I asked him *why* he was scratching up pictures of his mother. He said he didn't scratch up pictures of his mother—the wall did it.

"I'm sixty-five years old, and I've never seen a wall scratch up a picture—so you're lying," I said. "If you're lying, you're lying to cover up a truth. Don't be afraid of me; tell me the truth."

The boy burst into tears. "I miss my father!" he said.

His sister was molested by his father. He was torn between the memories of a father who didn't do anything to him except love him, and the loyalty to a mother and sister who were traumatized. Children often don't have the emotional aptitude or language to find the words to express what they are going through, so they become disruptive and destructive. He was frustrated because he couldn't express his guilt for loving somebody the rest of the family has decided he's not supposed to love. That spoke to me in a powerful, profound way. There was so much going on in that house. When drama breaks loose in a house, the people who end up most affected are the ones with the least power.

Martin Luther King Jr. once said, "A riot is the language of the unheard."

I thought of that when I listened to the boy; he was rioting because he was unheard. I created an environment where he could be heard. In his case, we needed to separate dysfunction from disruption and give him permission to be confused. The whole family was confused. Why would we expect an eight-year-old to just go over to the corner and play with his toys and not notice his family is in utter chaos? That was the reality going on behind closed doors. And we find those closed doors in every kind of family and community imaginable. You can't teach over trauma. You can't talk over trauma. You can't pay over trauma. No matter how much money or power or fame or prestige you have, the trauma is going to find a way to the surface.

When we put a seed in the ground, we expect it to be disruptive, to burst through the soil and grow. It's going to disrupt the environment around it. Because disruption is growth. When the human body grows, it breaks through its clothes—all of a sudden, Trey's pants don't fit anymore. We call them growing pains. Whether our budget can handle it or not, the boy still needs new sneakers. We can't stop him from growing until we get a raise. Every parent has to decide at some point: *What do we value most, the ham or the pan? Are we tethered to our way, or can we allow some room for a different way?*

My mother was a strong, educated, stereotypically tough Black woman who was determined to raise amazing children. She and my sister used to butt heads all the time. My mother was not the type of parent to let you talk back or snort or make a sound when you walked away; she'd call you out with a quickness. One day she and my sister had gotten into it once again, and my sister stomped up the stairs while saying something smart under her breath. My mother let her go and didn't respond, which was totally out of character. I was shocked. Since I was the baby of the family, I had access to her in a way other people didn't.

"Why didn't you say anything?" I asked her. "You always say something."

She turned to me and said, "Sometimes, son, you can win the battle and lose the war."

When it comes to disruptive children, sometimes as a parent we have to sacrifice the battle to win the war. No matter the size of our ego, the rigidity of the pan—the system we operate in—or how loyal we are to how we were raised, at some point we have to choose the ham or the pan. That means we have to lose some battles to win the war.

If we're invested in using whatever means we find necessary to squelch any dissent and stop them from talking back and expressing themselves, that doesn't mean their feelings and opinions will go away. We might have repressed it, but it's going to pop up somewhere else—and we don't get to pick where that might be. Once I plant a vine, I can stop it from coming straight up by putting a cinder block over it—but every gardener knows that vine is going to find its way to the surface somewhere else.

When I was in my thirties, I was really frustrated by some of the things my sons were doing when they were fully in the throes of the knucklehead stage. Y'all know exactly the stage I'm talking about, when it appears that the boy has truly misplaced every ounce of sense he might have had. I was ranting about their behavior—even though I really wasn't going to do anything.

"If they keep running down this road they're on, I'm gonna put them out!" I said in a bluster-filled tirade to my spiritual father.

He looked at me. "Put them out to what?" he said. "If you put them out, you can't control who picks them up. And if they pick them up, you're still gonna have the same problem to deal with."

Too many contemporary parents, in my view, have underestimated the difficulty of parenting. It is a helluva lot harder than what we watched on TV. It is an unscripted drama—and we grew up watching scripted shows. Not only that, it is an unscripted drama that never really ends. If we're still alive, we can't ever really say we're through. My oldest children are in their forties, and if they get sick, if they get hit by a car, if a drunk driver hits them, if they are the drunk driver, I'm still getting out of that bed. Even if I've got a cane and a walker, I'm getting out of that bed. The child might have grown, but it's still my child. The job never ends. It changes, but it's never over. They may become less dependent, more capable, and more assertive, but because life is so tempestuous, there will be moments of grave darkness when we are the only source of unconditional love. Even though they may resent us, criticize us, or try to ignore us, they will always need us. There is no retirement. There may be a point where they need our ear more than our mouth. Our job is to be instinctive enough to figure out when that point has come—and shut up.

We can't protect them from the shock. We can't control what the shocks will be and when they will come. Sometimes we won't even know when the shocks come. But we must take solace in this: the same God that carried us through our darkest hour and enabled us to become who we are does not have grandchildren, only children. And we have to trust Him to help us raise a disruptive thinker, whether that child ends up a genius or a janitor. Or a genius who's a janitor. Even if we're believing and trusting through a flood of tears, we have to keep believing. And trusting.

TWELVE

WHAT WE MUST DO NOW

I was in New York one day at an event being held in my honor by one of the executives at Goldman Sachs, a woman named Lisa Opoku, who is a partner at Goldman Sachs and the global head of the Goldman Sachs Partner Family Office, which provides wealth management services to the company's current and former partners and managing directors. The room was packed with impressive, high-level Black executives from the company, who were getting up and telling their stories. The energy in the room was palpable and exciting. When Leke Osinubi—the chief digital risk officer for Goldman Sachs and the chief information security officer for Goldman Sachs Bank USA—rose and told of his journey, I was blown away.

Osinubi grew up in a Nigerian family of engineers. When he was a teenager, he became enamored of sneakers, but he knew his very practical Nigerian parents would never give him the kind of cash he'd need to get his hands on the latest, trendiest sneakers. When he got to college and started delving into tech, he discovered that most companies had websites that were vulnerable to hacking. He figured out a way to hack into the sites of sneaker companies—and have the latest, hottest sneakers diverted to him. Finally, he had in his possession every sneaker he ever dreamed of owning. He began marketing and selling them, earning enough money to buy a brand-new car.

That's where his tech journey began, stealing some sneakers. Now, he oversees digital risk for one of the most esteemed financial companies in the world.

When I heard Osinubi's story, I walked away with a powerful thought: *It does not matter where you start; it matters where you finish.*

As we come to the close of this book, each person who reads these pages will be standing in a different place. Some will be at the beginning of their journey. Some will be in the middle—which may be the hardest place because it often feels so nebulous, neither the start nor the finish. The middle is the twilight song of becoming, the hazy dusk before the moon shines brightest. The final group is reading after they've already stepped into the discomfiting embrace of disruption.

To each person, no matter where you are on your journey, I say this: *keep moving.*

Whether you just discovered yourself from stealing tennis shoes, whether you are stuck in the middle of the jarring leap over the wall—with pain so intense that you're wondering whether it was even worth it to leap—or whether you've landed on the other side of something that is so unfamiliar that you don't even know what to call it, *keep moving.* You may have worked yourself into a room for which you have no point of reference, no experience to understand. You may be sitting in a place that looks magical, that feels transcendent, but is almost too good to believe. *Is this truly me?* you may be asking yourself, as you fight off impostor syndrome. Regardless, *keep moving.*

If you stay there long enough, foreigners become citizens. Immigrants become leaders. We're all immigrants during the first stage of crossing over the fence. But if you work hard enough, if you own it, if you don't run away from it, eventually the system will embrace you. You will become one of them. You will belong.

If you must, reach out for help along the way. Cry if you feel it's necessary. Don't be afraid. A friend once told me this: Tenacity will get you there. Consistency will keep you there. Gratefulness will give you more of what's there.

Keep moving.

DISRUPTIVE THINKING ESSAYS

OSCAR WILLIAMS

"Offer accepted!"

These were the words I said to my Realtor after she disclosed an offer from a California couple embarking upon their new journey in Dallas, Texas. This young husband and wife fell in love with my two-story traditional brick home situated in a quaint and established suburban Dallas neighborhood. Accepting that offer would open the door to repositioning myself financially and start my path toward wealth building. However, putting myself in a position to say those words meant challenging and changing my thought process—or, better put, disruptive thinking.

It started with a disruptive question. "Do I really want to own a home?" After being an avid renter with a nonchalant ideology surrounding home ownership, my thinking shifted when we entered the year 2020. That question sparked other questions, such as "What am I afraid of?" and "What is hindering me from stepping into home ownership?" It wasn't the challenge or the responsibility that made me shy away; the real culprit holding me back was me. I had become a bit complacent and reluctant to disrupt my norm. Complacency can sometimes be disguised as safety. Wouldn't we love to lead a life where our decisions always made us feel safe? Unfortunately, this is often not the case. Disruption can cause discomfort, but it doesn't mean you won't make it to your destination. Imagine cruising at thirty thousand feet in the air and suddenly the pilot comes on and says, "There's been a disruption to the flight plan, and we have to reroute, but we will still get to our destination." This is the equivalent of disruptive thinking. It interrupts your regularly scheduled program to offer an alternative that sometimes proves to be the change that you need.

I remember having a conversation with Bishop Jakes and being challenged with the thought of throwing more at the future me than what I was splurging on the present me. What would the older me need that the younger me has the resources and energy to supply? I realized that I had not prepared for anything beyond the moment I was standing in. And that's when the disruptive question mounted to a disruptive thought: "I am going to buy a house in a pandemic."

One thing that has been consistent with me is when I lock on to something mentally, I become ferocious and tenacious until I get what I set out to get. I began to research geographic areas and the Dallas housing market. I wanted to know neighborhood trends and local cities that were on a trajectory upward. I studied to be prepared to negotiate and get the best for my money. I started working on my debt and understanding mortgage terms that would affect financial outcomes. Things seemed to be flowing well. I looked at homes that I instantly fell in love with. I figured the process would be a breeze. I found a friendly lender who courted me until I was completely sold on their product. Finally, I would be a homeowner in about thirty days.

That is until I ran into the giant of all giants. His name was Credit! I never really knew why when I was nineteen my father told me, "Son, don't max out that credit card. Be wise with your use of it." Oh, how I wish I had hearkened to those words. It wasn't that I had bad credit; I just didn't understand how credit worked. I didn't know that credit used unwisely will lead you to an endless cycle of mounting debt that will ultimately hinder your buying power. I also didn't know that having a certain credit score can cost you thousands of dollars, literally. As you can imagine, no success story is unaccompanied by a series of failures. That oh-so-friendly lender quickly became "gone with the wind" when it seemed that my credit and debt-to-income ratio would ultimately stand in the way of my dream home and the bank's sizable commission. I guess I would return to the comfort of renting and set aside the idea of ownership. This is where the disruptive thought turned to disruptive thinking.

Disruptive thinking is a concept that spans past just a thought and interrupts your whole thought process. This type of thinking forced me to become creative and learn from every no that I encountered. The first thing I did was become a licensed loan officer. As if I didn't have enough degrees, disruptive thinking said to me, "If you want to know what they know, know what they know." So, I enrolled in an online course, passed my online studies, took the Texas state loan officer license test, and passed on the first try. Now, I could speak and understand the terms offered but also know my options. The rejection from the lender pushed me to examine my credit profile and seek help from professionals about how to employ the credit that I had to work for me.

It took me a few months, but with diligent work and education I increased my credit score to a place where I would be in optimal standing for the best mortgage rate there was. I also found time to explore more geographic areas and look deeper into what I wanted in a house and neighborhood. *Equity* became my new catchword. That disruptive thinking had me turning my gaze from the pretty landscape and hardwood floors to appraised value and negotiating the selling price. Learning the lesson that all home sales are not built equally but are built on equity was golden. Finally, I remembered the adage "There is more than one fish in the sea." In this case, there was more than one lender willing to work with my scenario and offer what I needed. I had to find a lender that wanted to be my partner and not just push their product. Doing my due diligence to explore which partner would work best for what I was trying to achieve provided me with a lender that offered the right loan program and consistent help along the way. They were so impressed with my knowledge that after I got my loan, they offered me a job as well. But that's another story for another time.

All of these lessons led me to purchase my first home in the middle of a pandemic, walking in the door with $30,000 of equity in the home. But better than that, just about a year later, I was able to say those two precious words that would allow me to walk away from that property with almost double what I paid for it. Offer accepted!

OSCAR WILLIAMS JR. *is a native of St. Louis, Missouri, currently residing in Dallas, Texas. He holds a bachelor's degree in music, a master's degree in music composition, and a doctoral degree in educational leadership and management. He is the pastor of arts and worship at the Potter's House Church of Dallas. Dr. Williams also serves as CEO and president of Speak Life LLC; CEO of Speak Life Academy of Arts and Music, Inc.; adjunct professor at Trevecca University; advisory board member at Jakes Divinity School; and cultural ambassador with the US State Department. He is a composer, artist, and writer.*

TRISTAN WALKER

My wife urged me to see a doctor.

Without any clear reason, I suddenly had an intense pain in my shoulder. I had no idea what that pain could be. It was nothing I had experienced before, and I was having trouble even describing it. The year was 2018. I sat down at the doctor's table, we greeted each other, and I explained to her how and what I was feeling. Within a few seconds, it was clear that she recognized my symptoms.

"Have you ever contracted chicken pox?" she asked.

"Yes, when I was six," I replied.

She paused, and with a more concerned voice and a furrowed brow, she asked, "How old are you?"

I replied, "I'm thirty-four."

She shook her head and gave me the diagnosis. "You have shingles," she said.

"I have what?"

I had never heard of shingles. The look on my face must have been one of shock and concern. Fortunately, her manner was kind, and with a most reassuring response she let me know that as far as the pain was concerned, a simple pain relief medication would clear it up quickly.

Now came the more important conversation. The fact that I had shingles at my age was a big concern. While one in three people will contract shingles in their lifetime, it is most commonly diagnosed for people over fifty. For someone my age, symptoms generally only surfaced under situations of significant chronic stress. It was the first time in my life that I recognized that my body and my mind were telling me two different things. I didn't *feel* stressed, but I *was* stressed. My mind was trying to convince me that I was handling things. My body disagreed. The urgent trip to the doctor was a warning sign. It was time for change during a trying season of transition.

At the time, my company's impact on our industry was lauded, our revenues were growing, and my family's support was as strong as it had ever been. In the coming months, my wife and I expected to welcome our second child, August, to the world. Meanwhile, I struggled to raise money for my company to fuel its growth, and as a result, we had to reduce our workforce by almost half. At the same time, I considered moving my family and company to a new city. The constant chatter in my mind debated whether this would be a season that explodes with opportunities for bounty, hope, and joy, or a stormy season of uncertainty and pain. Not knowing the answer for sure, I could only rely on my faith for answers to present themselves.

The first of my core values, "Have faith," gave me the courage to stay true, model the way for myself and others, and inspire action with objectivity and consistency. My remaining values encourage me to be courageous (and boldly persist), to inspire authentically, to show respect, to engage with good judgment and prudence, to choose wellness, and to earn loyalty. I further reasoned that the future I had in mind could never be seen clearly without faith as a guide. My second step would require releasing my burden of selfishness. Therapy would help provide guidance, perspective, and insight to help me define and understand the root causes of my stressors and why I chose selfishness as a sword and a shield: I carried a heavy and self-imposed burden of expectations for commercial success.

Generating significant financial wealth and receiving recognition for the work our company had done signaled success, but these were undefined vanity metrics, of which I could never have enough. The press wasn't enough. The authentic plaudits the company had received for our impact on the industry weren't enough. Our company's revenue growth wasn't enough. My growing financial balance sheet wasn't enough. I wanted more.

The pride in our work that had served me so well became a burden that grew heavier and heavier. The whispers grew louder and louder, until I could finally hear them shout that shame-inducing lyric from the poet Paul Laurence Dunbar (when the children laughed at Ole Uncle Hiram Dane when he belittled the value of educators teaching children to spell, and he couldn't even spell the word *charity* himself) that "Pride walks in slipp'ry places."

Now came the understanding. The burden of desire for more would prove unsustainable. I also learned three more things: First, my own suffering is neither special nor unique; it is shared. Second, in times of stress and duress, we can get through those times with continuous reflection and decision-making shaped by our personal values. And finally, seasons end. Good seasons end. Bad seasons end. The cycle repeats, and that's guaranteed. Equipped with that tool kit of reflection and understanding of shared suffering, modeled values, and the transcendency of seasons, I would be empowered to act.

No longer laden with worry, I built the courage to immediately right-size the business to set us up for sustained growth. We engaged in conversations with multiple large companies that signaled a strong interest in partnering with us to scale the inspired work we were doing, and within three months, our season of stress had given way to the next: we merged with Procter & Gamble, whose net sales in 2018 surpassed $66 billion. I became the first Black CEO of a subsidiary within the enterprise's 180-year history. Our loyal, committed team members would have the potential to scale our impact to billions of people around the world. Procter & Gamble encouraged us to move our company and our families to Atlanta, where I was *already* planning to transition us, and a few months later, my wife and I welcomed our second son, August, to the world.

A good season would begin, but this time, with not only perspective and preparation, but also appreciation and respect for the impermanence of each season. I needed this disruption, the trial of illness, the trial of having to reduce my workforce, the trial of leading a team through a merger, and the trial of uncertainty. The experience was a reminder that the trials one goes through and the blessings he receives can be synonymous. We must "glory in tribulations also: knowing that tribulation worketh patience; and patience, experience; and experience, hope" (Rom. 5:3–4). I've lived it. I chose to let go of shame, ego, worry, and expectation, knowing that with surrender, the burden will be made lighter. Disruptive thinking requires one to take a first step. Most importantly, I know that each step toward faith will be less "slipp'ry" than the last, and for me, and for us, embracing our blessings, we must persist forward.

TRISTAN WALKER *is the founder and CEO of Walker & Company Brands. Walker also serves on the Foot Locker, Inc.; Shake Shack, Inc.; and Children's Healthcare of Atlanta boards of directors. Fortune magazine named him as one of fifty of the "World's Greatest Leaders." He has also been named a* USA Today *"Person of the Year" and listed as one of* Time's 100 Next, Ebony Magazine's *100 Most Powerful People,* Vanity Fair's *"Next Establishment,"* Fortune *magazine's "40 Under 40,"* AdAge's *"Creative 50," and* Black Enterprise's *"40 Next." He is also the founder of CODE2040, a program that matches high performing Black and Latino undergraduate and graduate coders and software engineering students with Silicon Valley start-ups for summer internships. Tristan holds a bachelor's degree in economics from Stony Brook University, where he graduated as valedictorian, and an MBA from the Stanford University Graduate School of Business. He currently lives with his wife, Amoy, and two sons, Avery and August, in Atlanta, Georgia.*

NONA JONES

I remember it like it was yesterday.

It was 2018, and my husband and I had been the senior leaders of our church in Gainesville, Florida, for three years, a church his father had founded almost forty years earlier. In addition to helping my husband serve our members as first lady and caring for our young children on weekends so he could attend members' weddings and funerals, I was also a leader of our praise team and served as director of our ladies ministry. Oh, one other important detail: I also held a full-time leadership role at a little start-up known as Facebook that required weekly travel to business meetings around the United States and world.

It was commonplace for me to spend my work-week somewhere in the US, then take a flight back to Gainesville on Thursday in order to land at 6:35 p.m. and race to church for praise team rehearsal at seven. I routinely held planning meetings with our ladies' ministry leadership team via Zoom because I was in London or Australia or Egypt. I remember calling members immediately after landing in California or

Texas or New York to offer biblical counsel or pray with them due to a personal crisis. But all of that still wasn't enough . . . *for her.*

"I'm leaving the church," she told my husband.

"Leaving? Why?" he asked.

"I just can't stay at a church where the first lady is so . . . not involved," she responded.

"What do you mean by that?" he said.

"Well, she was supposed to fill in for me and lead worship a few Sundays, but had to back out because she was traveling somewhere. It just seems like she has other priorities, and that doesn't work for me," she said.

My husband thanked her for telling him, then texted me with the news. "Janice says she's leaving because . . . you have a job."

Janice was the leader of our praise team, so she held a highly visible role in our church. Her departure meant a major disruption to our praise team, because several of the members were her family or otherwise loyal to her. I knew that her decision to leave meant I would have to step in and lead the team because I was the co-leader.

As my plane sped down the runway and prepared to take off, I responded to my husband with the only thing I could muster: "Okay." I turned my phone on airplane mode . . . and sighed.

When my husband became a full-time pastor in October 2015, I assumed that I would fill the commonly accepted role of the first lady—sit in the front row of the church wearing a beautiful hat and offering a loving hug as people entered or exited the building. It seemed simple enough to me.

At the time of his installation, I served at the chief executive level of a major nonprofit organization and was working with the Obama White House to secure funding to expand the program nationally. Although I had to occasionally travel to Washington, DC, and Atlanta for meetings, it was sporadic, and I was a constant fixture at our church; wide-brimmed hat and lap scarf always in place while sitting in my front-row seat. But all of that changed on June 30, 2017.

I was driving home from West Palm Beach after attending the Leadership Florida Annual Meeting when my cell phone rang. It lit up with a 650 area code and a number I didn't recognize. I assumed it was a telemarketer and didn't plan to answer, but the Holy Spirit told me to take the call. To make a long story short, by the end of that call, I was offered the newly created role of head of faith-based partnerships at Facebook. Although I was told it had global scope, I naïvely assumed that I could fit a *global* role within the *local* expectations people had of their first lady, so I accepted it without a second thought. But as my job began to take me away more and more, I noticed an interesting reaction by some people, including Janice. They were okay with my influence expanding—as long as my expansion didn't require them to change.

I remember returning home from keynoting a conference in London, and I hadn't been able to attend rehearsal that week due to work. As I joined the team for soundcheck, the atmosphere of the team was noticeably sour. I mentioned it to Janice after service, and she simply rolled her eyes and said, "I don't know . . . I'm tired." I thought to myself, *Tired? I just took a red-eye flight to be here today, while you got a full night's rest.* Although I didn't verbalize the thought, I realized something in that moment that has stuck with me since that time.

Disruption that elevates you not only changes your circumstances; it also reveals which relationships can withstand the increased distance caused by your elevation. When my work allowed me to remain proximate to Janice, she was totally fine. But when my work increased the distance between us, she felt threatened by the separation and decided to walk away. I didn't know that at the time, and because I didn't, it took months of prayer and self-work to get to a healthy emotional state where I was no longer angry or hurt by her leaving. It also took a lot of time for me to stop blaming myself for her choice. I kept thinking, *Well, maybe if I had been there for rehearsal more, she would have stayed,* but I had to face the truth. Her decision to leave wasn't really about me. Her response was about her. When God decided to enlarge my territory, it wasn't because I applied for the job. It was because *He* decided to place me in it. As a result, the disruption was a divine appointment and necessarily required some pruning to take place in order to ensure my fruitfulness, according to John 15:2.

As I look back over that period, I realize that I was deeply insecure before my life was so radically disrupted. I wanted so badly to be approved by people and loved as first lady that I would often sacrifice my own well-being in hopes of making them happy. But after realizing that people will *still* walk away from you, even after you give everything you have, I was freed to love people because *they* need to be loved, not because I need to be loved in order to feel worthy.

Today I am still first lady of our church, and I am still leader of our worship team. I am still leading the global faith-based partnerships team at Facebook, and my role has expanded to include even more functions over the years. But there is one thing that I am *not*: I am not willing to shrink my purpose down so that it fits within the too-small confines of other people's opinions. Disruption not only changes your situation; it also changes the composition of the supporting cast in your life. And, though painful in the moment, it is *always* for the better.

NONA JONES *is a rare combination of preacher, business executive, author, and entrepreneur. Her corporate leadership includes serving as the head of global faith-based partnerships at Meta, the company formerly known as Facebook; chief external affairs officer for a multistate school for at-risk girls; and public policy director for a multiservice utility company. She is the best-selling author of three books and has been profiled by* Essence Magazine *as an "Under 40 Woman to Watch" and* Florida Trend *magazine as one of Florida's "30-Something All-Stars." She and her husband pastor Open Door Church in Gainesville, Florida.*

KEION HENDERSON

At its core, disruptive thinking is any process or thought that challenges your traditional ways of reasoning. I think that it is important to stress that disruptive thinking doesn't necessarily mean dangerous thinking or destructive thinking. Disruptive thinking in this context just means different. It means taking the risk of being misunderstood in the eyes of the people who formed your thinking, while knowing that you'll soon be affirmed by those who experience it.

Recently, while taking my daughter to school on a cool rainy morning, she looked on the display screen of my car and saw the icon of an iPod. She said to me with such purity, "Daddy, my teacher showed me one of those today in class. I saw one of those in real life." She described it as though it were a dinosaur. If you are near my age or older—which is forty-one at the time of this writing—an iPod in the early 2000s represented a technological breakthrough and advancement that rivaled space exploration technology. Not really, but you get the picture. There is no doubt that it represented disruptive thinking. Most people went from having twenty to thirty compact discs in an overstretched sleeve above the sun visor to having music at our fingertips.

Who would have ever thought that it was possible that you could have thousands of songs on one device that could fit in your pocket? But nothing stays the same, now does it? Now the iPod has been combined with the iPhone, and we all have thousands of songs, multiple apps, hundreds of contacts, thousands of text messages, a flashlight, a camera, and hundreds of gigabytes of information all living in one device that fits in the same pocket. That's what disruptive thinking is: combining what was and adding to it what is. It's the process of improving on what was once known as the best and attempting to make it better. If you are interested in getting everything out of you that is within you, this is exactly the type of thinking you will have to exercise.

It was at this crossroads that the biggest economic shift of my life began. All of my life I've been taught to go to school, get a job, make as much money as you can, live off 70 percent, put 10 percent in a savings account, tithe 10 percent, and invest 10 percent. Please don't misunderstand me—it's a good strategy. But I have now learned that it is nowhere close to being disruptive.

After recently attending a meeting with several billionaires and multiple multimillionaires, I was afforded the opportunity to gain insight on disruptive thinking up close and personal. That disruptive thinking came in the area of real estate acquisition. This meeting sparked the thinking that led to the action that put my new mindset into practice and changed my tax bracket. Most of you reading this will be able to empathize with this idea of going to work, saving your money, buying a house, and paying it off. It has been and still is a part of the fabric of the American dream. It may be a dream, but it's far from disruptive. What if I told you there is a disruptive way, a way that's controversial but works?

I recently got married and sought to take out a jumbo loan to buy myself and my beautiful wife the home of our dreams. You know the one: the ten-to-fifteen-thousand-square-foot house on the two-to-five-acre plot of land, equipped with a swimming pool, tennis court, and basketball court. The plan was to buy the house in a great neighborhood, make sure it was well maintained, and hopefully (emphasis on *hopefully*) in the next ten to fifteen years sell the property for profit and either put the proceeds and equity toward a retirement home or retirement account.

I was approved for the loan as a regular thinker, but by the time I was given the money, I had already become a disruptive thinker. It was too late; my perspective had shifted. And because I am now a disruptive thinker, I changed the direction of the flow of the currency. Disruptive thinking said take the same money and buy real estate—not a single-family dwelling, but a multi-family unit that produces passive income (rent)—and allow the passive income to pay the rent on the place where my wife and I now live. According to ABC13.com, rent in the city where I live will increase

23 percent over the next seven years. The same outlet is also reporting that America is nearing a recession amid recent inflation.

This equation is why the disruptive strategy is the smart strategy. Passive income, from rental real estate, is not as subject to high effective tax rates or market downturns, but equity on a single dwelling home is. The income from my rental real estate is sheltered by the appreciation and amortization, and results in a much lower effective tax rate. Passive income beats earned income all day as a result of this.

If my grandfather were alive, he'd probably call me an idiot for not owning my home. However, I would know that he meant to call me disruptive. I would say, "Grandfather, one day I will own my own home. I am just allowing my tenants to buy it for me. I am now earning enough per month to cover 100 percent of my expenses off the investment. And I am not waiting on a bull or bear market to inform me of how much my equity is worth."

In fact, disruptive thinking has left me with two responses as it relates to the market: in a good market, raise the rent, and in a bad market, raise the rent.

Best-selling author and treasured spiritual leader KEION D. HENDERSON *is the founder, CEO, and senior pastor of the Lighthouse Church and Ministries, one of America's fastest-growing churches, headquartered in Houston, Texas. His ministries and initiatives are fueling the explosive growth and far-reaching impact of the Lighthouse Church, whose congregation continues to blossom with more than fifteen thousand dedicated members and more than nine hundred thousand unique weekly viewers worldwide across all social media platforms. With over twenty-six years in active ministry, Pastor Henderson is known to educate, nurture, and equip his congregants with life-changing lessons to navigate their faith with sound values and biblical principles via his accelerator for entrepreneurship. Recognized by the John Maxwell Institute as one of the "Top 250 Leaders" in the nation, Pastor Keion Henderson, born in Gary, Indiana, is a devoted father to his beautiful daughter, Katelyn, and husband to his forever wife, Shaunie Henderson.*

DAVID L. STEWARD

Growing up Black comes with a unique set of disruptions, the most difficult of which is many times being judged simply by the color of one's skin instead of the content of one's character.

This is an unfortunate reality that persists even today. I am grateful to my parents for guiding me in the practical matters of life and instilling in me a love for God, His Word, and all His children. They taught me that hatred begets hatred, but God's love conquers all. My Christian faith has brought me to a point where I am seeking an "eternal return on investment" and working to leave a legacy rooted in faith.

Disruption started early in my childhood. I grew up on a small farm on the outskirts of Clinton, Missouri. We lived on the other side of the tracks in a segregated town, common for Black people in the 1950s. *Brown v. Board of Education* in 1954 meant that our town integrated its schools in 1957, the year I started first grade. The Ku Klux Klan was determined to put a halt to integration, declaring, "There's no way that is going to happen." My dad, however, was even more determined nothing would keep his children from receiving the education they deserved. So, he patrolled the town all night before the first day of school to make sure we would be safe. A father's love knows no bounds and conquers all fears.

I also saw the compassion my parents had for others. There were less fortunate men, or, as we called them back then, "hobos," who always came by our home near the railroad tracks. They did not look like us, but they were greeted with love by my family. I often wondered, "How do they find us?" My mom said our house was marked, and they knew they could receive food at our home. Now, we were as poor as church mice. With eight children to feed, it was rare for us to have leftovers. But Mom insisted that we give them what we had in our refrigerator, and they would sit on our back porch eating the much-needed meal.

Seeing this kindness, compassion, and love extended to strangers was a lesson that this life is about serving others. It is about making a difference in this world, regardless of one's ethnicity, education, or neighborhood.

It is about the condition of one's heart. Scripture tells us, "Whatever you have done for one of the least of these brothers and sister of mine, you did for me" (see Matt. 25:40 NIV). As my mom said often, "You might be the only Bible they see today." She extended the love of Jesus to everyone who came her way.

Disruption happened early in my business career.
As the first Black salesperson for FedEx, I received an award for top performer in 1981 and was given an ice bucket with my name engraved on it. As I looked into that empty ice bucket, it disrupted me. I yearned to be an entrepreneur like my dad, so I bought my own company, finding a way to automate and speed up freight bill audits for railroads and save them money.

Information technology was emerging as the next disruptive new thing. In 1990, my dream took shape, and the idea of World Wide Technology was born.

Those early years were tough and at times highly disruptive. Money went missing, we lost an important contract, the banks tried to shut us down, and my car was repossessed while I watched from an office window. Many of us worried the company might not make it, and that responsibility, along with the livelihood of my employees and their families, rested squarely on my shoulders.

There were times when I had to double down and prove that a Black man could lead a company in an industry where there was no one who looked like me. I had to work harder and be smarter and more innovative than my contemporaries. In the company's early days, when challenges abounded and money was tight, my mother-in-law called and encouraged me with the words of Psalm 91:2: The Lord is "my refuge and my fortress, my God, in whom I trust" (NIV). Her words of reassurance based on Scripture gave me the strength to keep moving forward with perseverance and determination.

With a great team, many of whom are still with the company today, we persevered beyond my wildest dreams. We survived, ultimately creating the largest Black-owned company in the United States, with $14.5 billion in sales and over ten thousand employees. World Wide Technology is the fulfillment of Ephesians 3:20: The Lord is "able to do immeasurably more than all we ask or imagine, according to his power that is at work within us" (NIV). Praise God for the amazing things He has done!!

What's next? More disruption.
This spirit of serving others instilled by my parents is one reason I am a longtime supporter of Concordance, a nonprofit organization dedicated to reducing reincarceration rates. This model is improving the quality of life for justice-involved men and women, their families, and our communities. The program offers a tremendous opportunity to disrupt a long-standing social and economic problem, especially in Black and brown communities, by addressing the horrific trauma most inmates have experienced beginning at a very young age.

Concordance helps reduce reincarceration rates by offering individuals recently released from prison a holistic program that presents a first real chance of healing from past traumas. The program focuses on treating substance abuse and mental health issues, job training and placement, and spiritual wholeness, in addition to other skills needed to lead a successful life. Reducing recidivism is critical to advancing racial equity in our country.

I am honored to chair the $100 million Concordance First Chance Campaign to expand the reach nationally and break the cycle of incarceration for generations to come.

On my path, there were many people who did not look like me yet helped light the path before me. I am eternally grateful to each one of them. It is my mission now to pay it forward, disrupting businesses and communities with technology that helps level the playing field for everyone, regardless of skin color, education, or socioeconomic background. I often ask myself, *Am I living a life worthy of the sacrifices made by those who have gone before me?*

The pain and the power of disruption gives us our ability to break the status quo and transform lives, communities, and the world.

DAVID L. STEWARD is the founder and chairman of World Wide Technology, an information technology systems integrator with $14.5 billion in annual sales and eight thousand employees. It is the largest

Black-owned company in the United States. Dave is committed to an eternal return on investment (EROI): "Trust in the Lord with all your heart and lean not on your own understanding; in all your ways submit to him, and he will make your paths straight" (Prov. 3:5–6 NIV).

DONNA RICHARDSON

When I was a little girl, I took a home economics class where I learned how to sew, crochet, knit, and quilt. I excelled in crocheting and knitting, and I decided in fourth grade to start my own business, because I didn't think my parents paid me enough allowance. I had a thriving business, but I learned early on about sacrifice when I couldn't have fun with my friends because there was work to be done. My first for-profit business venture closed many years ago, but today my love for crocheting allows me to bless others with designs created just for them.

When I started my fitness and wellness career in the late 1980s, traveling the world helping people become healthier, I discovered that my greatest challenge wasn't overseas—it was my family, my community, and my church. I became sick and tired of seeing loved ones suffering and dying from preventable illnesses. I adhered to the calling and became a change agent to eliminate the health disparities that existed in African American communities around the country. As I led the charge, I had no idea I was the first African American fitness and health expert with a prominent platform. I was a leading expert for national TV shows like *The Today Show* on networks such as NBC, ESPN, BET, TV One, and the Word Network, and starred in best-selling fitness videos like *Buns of Steel*, among others. I was inducted in the National Fitness Hall of Fame. I was also the spokesperson for household brands including the PGA, a board member for the LPGA Foundation, and former vice president for the Women's Sports Foundation, all while helping to create and promote my own signature shoe with Nike. I was the only council member appointed to serve on the President's Council for Sports, Fitness, and Nutrition for President George W. Bush and President Barack Obama. I was also honored to teach for several years at the Oprah Winfrey Leadership Academy in South Africa. I was a "first" in the fitness and health industry, but I had the responsibility to reach back and help others.

Early in 2020, before the pandemic hit, I enjoyed being a motivational speaker and a consultant for churches, corporations, and community centers. I was completing items on my "It's Possible" list while living a purposeful life, including raising awareness and funds for causes dear to my heart. I climbed the largest free-standing mountain in the world, Mount Kilimanjaro; ran marathons; ran a two-hundred-mile relay race; and traveled to my fifty-first country. Then God shut the world down. In the midst of the pandemic, the loss of loved ones due to COVID-19, my mom's illness, my brother's two strokes, my back injury, and then a knee injury that left me barely able to walk, my eighty-one-year-old momma and I stepped out on faith and took our culturally rich family recipe to retail and restaurants. Although I was excited to embark on this new business, reality hit hard that the fitness and wellness business I'd run for thirty-five years was shut down. In hindsight, I can see that if the pandemic had not happened, we may not have our family business today.

For thirty years my mother, Mama LaVerne, had been traveling coast to coast cooking her award-winning chicken and waffles for family, friends, and celebrities. Once the pandemic happened, we couldn't get to them, and they couldn't come to us. We set up "Love Pickups" at our home so people could drive by and pick up our love meals. As the demand grew, we started mixing the ingredients and putting the mix in zip-lock bags and mailing it along with the recipe. As I was going through therapy and rehab so I can learn to walk again, we overcame obstacles and solved a problem. It was the birth of a family business. Our recipe is rooted in strength, courage, and resilience, and we turned our impossible to possible. Mama LaVerne's Chicken Seasoning Waffle and Pancake Mix is available online, in retail stores, and at restaurants, and it is popular for corporate gifting.

Because I had no income from my fitness and health business, I took out a loan and money from my retirement account to start our new business, Mama

LaVerne Foods. I became a student of the food industry. I did research, read books, and spoke with astute business owners like my pastor. I reached out to Michele Hoskins, who has been in the food industry for thirty-six years and is now my mentor. Even with a mentor I made mistakes along the way. Many sacrifices were made, including a failed relationship and missing out on family's and friends' events. I couldn't even travel, which is also one of my favorite passions, and so many other things I gave up. I worked around the clock, because this is truly a labor of love. This journey has taken me down roads with many twists and turns—being overstressed and riddled with anxiety, longing to be active again, shuffling to pay invoices, not having funds to increase brand awareness, not having funds for marketing and advertising, the difficulty of finding qualified and reliable workers once I could afford to hire staff, problems with a co-packer, the uncertainties and challenges of being in retail and restaurants. I have experienced complete exhaustion to the point that I fell asleep at the wheel while driving. To top it all off, last Christmas I was home and alone with COVID-19. There were so many more obstacles I had to overcome . . . but God! My radical faith and fight keep me pressing forward while experiencing the tribulations and triumphs. As the CEO of Mama LaVerne's Foods, my vision is to grow and scale the business to become a global lifestyle brand.

I stand on the shoulders of my ancestors. Every day I rise because they rose, I stand because they stood, and I fight because they fought. I have the faith of a mustard seed and the fortitude of those who came before me. I receive the baton, raise the bar, and will pass the baton to the next generation. What I learned in this journey is that it's worth the blood, sweat, tears, and a whole lot of pain. I trust the process. No matter what your age, circumstances, or limitations, you can achieve your goals and dreams. My mother as a little girl couldn't imagine that one day she would walk into Target and see her product grace the shelves of a major retailer or see her signature dish on the menu of one of Dallas's most prominent restaurants. My favorite pastor in the world once said, "Being relentless will get you there, being consistent will keep you there, and being grateful will increase what's there." When I wake up each morning it's about God, grace, gratefulness, and grind. As I evolve as a business owner in the fitness and food industry, this gives me an opportunity to serve at a greater level. I'm walking in my assignment. We are using our platform to give back to those in need, help eradicate hunger, and elevate humanity. Also, we are partnering with HBCUs for job opportunities with our company so we can invest in the future while growing our future.

As we spread love through food for the soul by putting love on your plate and joy in your tummy, I have become stronger and more determined than ever. I face fear and do it anyway. I have lost friends along the way, but they couldn't go with me where God is taking me. I don't worry about doubters or haters because their opinions are irrelevant to my purpose. I stay focused and obedient to God's plan, not my plan. Our core purpose is to enrich people's connections through food for the soul. Just like when I was a teenager and we gathered at my grandma's house after church for homemade food, fellowship, and fun, we hope to bring families and friends together to create sweet experiences and savory memories while enjoying delicious foods.

Looking back, I have been disruptive all my life: my first business venture was at age ten, then I had a fitness and wellness career nationally and internationally, and now my mom and I, at ages eighty-two and fifty-nine, launched the first ever chicken seasoning and waffle and pancake mix packaged together. As we walk by faith and not by sight, we keep hope because God says in Isaiah 43:18–19, "Do not remember the former things, nor consider the things of old. Behold, I will do a new thing, now it shall spring forth; shall you not know it? I will even make a road in the wilderness and rivers in the desert" (NKJV). We are living witnesses to the unlimited possibilities of disruptive thinking.

DONNA RICHARDSON *is a best-selling author, international motivational speaker, and TV host. She has traveled to fifty states, fifty countries, and six continents spreading the gospel of good health, mind, body, and spirit. Donna was named by* Essence Magazine *as*

"One of Twenty Five of the Most Inspiring Women in America." She received the Centennial Health Award from Delta Sigma Theta Sorority, its highest honor, and the Presidential Award from Alpha Kappa Alpha Sorority.

FREDERICK JOHNSON

My barber journey began with a nudge—rather inauspiciously, I might add. With a tiny razor blade, any man regardless of income or social status can be transformed into a debonair figure who exudes self-confidence.

That desire to achieve a look that only a barber can provide prompted an older relative to ask me, a teenager at the time, to cut his hair. With a nonadjustable clipper and a box of single-edge razor blades, I proceeded to give him a college cut and edge-up as he coached me through the process. But even with his guidance, I couldn't shake the nervousness that comes with doing something so significant for the first time. While lining his hair, the blade slipped through my moist hands and cut him across the forehead. But even with blood running down his face he remained in the chair. Knowing the value of a good haircut, he encouraged me to keep going, and I completed the job. When I finished, he put his arms around me and told me, "Job well done." I walked away knowing two things: First, I found out a man loved me enough to bleed for me. Second, I realized I had found my life's purpose. From that day forward, with a razor blade, I could change a person's appearance while carving out a career of my own.

I honed my skills in high school by cutting hair whenever there was an opportunity. All I needed was a razor blade and soap and water to completely enhance the appearance of my clients. By my senior year at Humphreys County High School, I was so advanced that I could create graffiti-style designs in my peers' heads while sitting in the classroom. I knew I had a gift; it was now up to me to pursue the dream and take it to the next level.

Upon graduating in 1993, I joined the military and took them up on their promise to pay for my college education. After obtaining a license in barbering school, I opened my first barbershop in my hometown, Belzoni, Mississippi. Being a hometown hero and serving as an inspiration to the next generation was quite an achievement. However, I had my eyes on bigger goals and knew that I needed to display my barbering skills on a larger scale. With only a few dollars and a dream, I packed my bags and my favorite razor blades and moved to Dallas.

I soon found out that everything is big in Texas, including the obstacles. Without many connections in Dallas at the time, I discovered that it was difficult to find a barber shop that was the right fit for my personality and skill set. To take a step forward, I needed to take a step back.

Although I possessed the talent to be one of the best barbers in Texas, my time had yet to arrive. I decided to enroll in school to receive HVAC training and began a career as an A/C technician. The new occupation allowed me to gain a steady income and stability in my personal life. I got married, had kids, and built a house. I would still cut hair in my garage at times, but it wasn't the same as owning my shop and building a brand. Following the 9/11 attacks, I was released by my employer and given a severance package. The severance was the boost I needed to get back into the business of barbering full-time.

But this time around, I had a plan. I could no longer exist as just another barber. I needed to approach the business as if my life depended on it. I found a way to disrupt the industry.

It all began with the work. I had to invest in myself first. I wanted to stand out by doing things the average barber could not fathom. My shop needed to be a place where every man could feel like a distinguished gentleman. It would start with the barber's chair.

In the South, there's a certain admiration for vintage items. Old-school cars (vehicles that are usually more than thirty years old) are often transformed into sleek automobiles with glistening paint jobs, shiny rims, and refurbished engines. I took that same approach with barber chairs. I would search for vintage barber chairs and, if needed, would take flights across the nation to purchase them. To get the barber chairs back to Texas, I would dismantle them, have each part shipped, and reconstruct the chair once back home. And then the fun would begin. I would add my personal touch by adding items such as ostrich leather and chrome and candy-color paint to the barber chairs. The process would cost me thousands of dollars and time away from family, but the investment proved to be worth every penny.

Another step I took to disrupt the barbering industry was to brand myself. I began participating in barber competitions and embraced a name that represented my hometown and aspects of my skills. In a sense, great barbers perform surgery on their clients, enhancing their appearance to the point where they can feel like a new man. I reintroduced myself as Sipp the Surgeon and never looked back.

When competing against other barbers, I added theatrics to my show. My wardrobe would be immaculate, my razors would be extra sharp, and every viewer would be entertained.

I named my home base the Art of Barbering, the most exquisite barber shop in Dallas, complete with a granite bar, metallic epoxy floors, flat-screen TVs in every room, and eighteen different vintage barber chairs that each featured a custom theme.

I've had the opportunity to groom A-list clients from all walks for life. Hip-hop royalty including Emmy-nominated super producer Adam Blackstone, Drake, DJ Khaled, Rick Ross, Kendrick Lamar, Bryson Tiller, YG, Tyga, Young Dolph, Lil Twist, Dorrough, and Hollyhood Bay Bay—the man who kept the world dancing during a global health crisis. And Touré Roberts, a renowned man of faith.

Nationally, my profile grew with an appearance on *Cedric's Barber Battle*, hosted by Cedric the Entertainer. I demonstrated the haircut with a chainsaw and won $15,000. I was invited to the biggest barbering competition, the seventieth anniversary Bronner Bros. International Beauty Show, and I won a $10,000 cash prize in their competition. Soon after, I was featured in a national AT&T/NBA season-opening commercial featuring NBA legends Magic Johnson, Dirk Nowitzki, and Megan Thee Stallion. As a result of this national recognition, SCurl presented me with an opportunity to become a global ambassador.

Ultimately, I was featured on the cover of *Barber Evo*, the most sought-after barbering magazine in North America, and traveled throughout the United Kingdom and Ireland twice. My name continued to grow nationally, but some of the most important relationships would come from local connections.

Through one of my VIP clients in Dallas, I was introduced to Bishop T.D. Jakes. In our first encounter, I provided him with a shave that went beyond the average haircut. I eventually became his personal barber. Having the opportunity to serve as the main barber for one of the world's biggest disrupters changed my life. We developed a great relationship beyond the chair, often partnering in ventures such as the MegaFest Hair

Battle. As our bond grew, I became more intrigued by the methods he used to inspire millions from the pulpit. When I listened to his sermons, I would get chills. I wanted to know how he found a way to muster up the strength to influence the masses through his ministry. He told me that once you know your craft, you can be amazing and influence others as well. To have the trust of one of the most revered leaders of this generation continues to be empowering in my professional and personal life.

Along the way, I've missed ball games, recitals, dinners, and a host of other outings I can't recall. Each time, no matter what I missed, the missing part was done with an eye toward building the ones who matter most—family—a brighter tomorrow. It was a high cost to pay, but I'm blessed to be surrounded by people who share in the vision of success that was imparted to me many, many years ago. Their unwavering support has been an integral part of my success, and for that I'm eternally grateful.

My journey to success has not been linear. From the first day I picked up a razor to cut a relative's hair in a small town in Mississippi to winning national barbering competitions, my achievements would not be possible without finding ways to think outside of the box. There are millions of barbers around the world. But the few who can stand out in a crowded field only do so by embracing disruptive thinking.

When I sit back and think about the journey I've traveled thus far and the many miles I'm believing God to carry me through, I'm humbled by the fact that it all began because two men—one up above and one down here below—loved me enough . . . to bleed.

FREDERICK JOHNSON, *aka Sipp the Surgeon, has been a licensed barber for over twenty-five years, winning several barber championships along the way becoming the trusted barber to many high-profile celebrities. He currently serves as an SCurl global ambassador and has been involved with behind-the-scenes grooming for magazine covers, television commercials, and music video shoots. Sipp has been featured in national television commercials, most recently the AT&T Codes of Culture campaign. As the owner of a premier barbershop in Grand Prairie, Texas, called the Art of Barbering, Sipp the Surgeon will continue to cut hair with surgical precision.*

CHRISTOPHER LYONS

Throughout my journey in the technology industry, I have learned that the best companies and ideas are built from disruptive thinking. The contrarian mindset provides the opportunity to look beyond current market conditions and envision an alternative approach that could provide exponential value to an industry unaware of needing change. Less than ten years ago, the thought of staying in a stranger's home instead of a hotel, or driving in the back seat of a stranger's car, would've been considered crazy. Yet businesses like Uber, Lyft, and Airbnb have completely shifted our perspectives and revolutionized the transportation and hospitality industries.

Every person has an ordained "earned secret" that brings a divine perspective toward a solvable problem that only *you* have the unique insight to solve. I began my career in the music and entertainment industry, yet I was always passionate and fascinated by how software and technology impacted the world. I noticed how revolutionary the smartphone would be in all sectors and decided to move to Silicon Valley to pursue my first technology start-up, PictureMenu. The journey of building my company ultimately led me into venture capital, where I landed a position as chief of staff at Andreessen Horowitz.

While I knew that coming from a different industry would be difficult, I also knew that my understanding of cultural innovation could be an asset to Silicon Valley. I leaped toward the opportunity to explore the world of start-ups and venture capital. I was often the only Black man in the room and dove headfirst into complex topics focused on finance and computer science. There were many situations at the beginning of my career in tech where I felt outside my comfort zone. Still, I quickly learned that the feeling of insecurity was actually fuel to harness a new level of disruptive thinking.

My mind began integrating disruptive thinking to solve the problem that culture and technology leaders needed to work more closely together. I discovered that consumer technology companies like Instagram, Pinterest, and Snap were growing at extreme rates due to the massive engagement of strategic influencers on their platform. Yet, these entrepreneurs never had the opportunity to participate in the equity upside of the business despite their content being the reason behind the company's increase in valuation. Black culture has also always been the leading indicator for consumer trends (sports, music, fashion, art, and now consumer technology) and needed to be better represented on the cap tables of these companies.

With that in mind, I began constructing a way to pioneer both verticals into a new venture capital fund within Andreessen Horowitz called the Cultural Leadership Fund (CLF). By bridging these two worlds, CLF introduced the venture capital asset class to the world's greatest athletes, entertainers, musicians, and senior-level executives. In 2018, this group of limited partners became the first fund in the history of Silicon Valley to comprise 100 percent of Black investors. As this strategic network began working with the world's greatest technology companies, their brand of innovation also began to advance, providing win-win partnerships. Bridging Silicon Valley's genius with the genius of CLF's influencer network brought a cultural change to venture capital, alongside new access and opportunity within the technology industry.

Creating CLF was one of the most challenging projects I've ever embarked on. Launching the first fund was *not* easy, and it made me realize that to see your vision come to life, you will have to overcome multiple hurdles along the way. You must constantly adapt to the problems before finding your way to the next objective. When it feels like all options have been exhausted, always remember that there *is* a move.

CLF has raised three funds since 2018 with over $70 million in assets under management. There are more than three hundred Black investors now integrated into the venture capital ecosystem, where we've syndicated over $20 million in individual capital into some of the world's most innovative technology companies. Most importantly, the fund's management fees and carry will be redistributed back to a select number of nonprofits advancing the next generation of Black and brown leaders through technical skills.

Disruptive thinking begins with the decision to disrupt your doubts, disrupt the mental blocks telling you what isn't possible, disrupt the current environment that seems too difficult to get out of, and disrupt any cognitive evidence of fear or insecurity. Once you break through the first layer of disruptive thinking (which is yourself), you realize that whatever you want to accomplish is already waiting on the other side, ready for you to materialize.

CHRISTOPHER LYONS *is the president of web3 media at a16z crypto. Prior to joining the team at a16z crypto, he cofounded the firm's Cultural Leadership Fund and was instrumental in launching the first seed fund. Lyons started his career in the music industry working for Grammy Award–winning producer Jermaine Dupri as a sound engineer. He then launched his first start-up, a mobile app and digital menu offering called PictureMenu. Lyons is on the advisory boards of the Black Economic Alliance and New Story as well as a member of the Verizon Media Global Advisory Board. Lyons is the founder of Italian wine brand Lyons Wine, a Kauffman Fellows graduate (class of '19), and a member of Kappa Alpha Psi Fraternity, Inc. (KT spring '07). Lyons received a bachelor of science degree in entertainment business from Full Sail University in 2010.*

JANICE BRYANT HOWROYD

There have been many opportunities for disruption to support my life and, thus, those around me. Most people think of the disruption in my business and industry when they associate this with me. Some think of my communities or my work around social and economic discipleship. At this stage in my life, yes, disruption has been ripe and fruitful. Thinking on this at the deepest part of my life, though, it is truly changing the *how* of how I have seen myself that has been the strongest disrupter in my life.

Mind you, it is not the "what I have done" nor simply the "who I want to be"; rather, the *how* of how I see myself. Not just how I see me. It's *how* I see how

I see myself. How I see myself allowed me to look at the physical of me. Addressing *how* I see how I see me has allowed me to look at the whole picture of my experience, which is inclusive of an awareness, as fully as possible, of environments, circumstance, and potentials around me.

It is not an arrival. It is a process and is iterative. Disrupting how I see how I see myself has supported me to break down denials, griefs, grudges, insecurities, and guilts. It has not served as a forgiveness platform; rather, it continues as a building and rebuilding platform. Praise God!

Born African American in the segregated town of Tarboro, North Carolina, JANICE BRYANT HOWROYD, *affectionately known as "JBH," is the first African American woman to found and build a multibillion-dollar company. The ActOne Group is a workforce solutions organization that operates in over thirty-four countries. It is engaging some of the world's best technologies and systems to support organizations of all sizes, and it facilitates jobs and careers for millions of workers across the globe. JBH has served on the White House–appointed Presidential Board of Advisors on Historically Black Colleges and Universities and the Federal Communications Commission's Advisory Committee on Diversity and Digital Empowerment, and she continues to serve on the ITAC 10 (International Trade Advisory Committee—Professional Services). She is chair of the*

Women's Leadership Board housed out of the Kennedy School of Government at Harvard University. She is an acclaimed author, speaker, and media personality. Asked how she continues to accomplish so much, she answers, "Faith is my foundation."

AARON JOHNSON

I'm called to be a disruptive thinker because I was disrupted, as far back as I can remember.

But God wanted my disruption to be someone else's breakthrough. I certainly didn't realize that as a child growing up in Milwaukee. I am the oldest son of Robert, a dynamic disrupter in his own right, a human resources manager who also pastored a small Church of God in Christ congregation. On the outside, we were the textbook church family: father, mother, three children—smart, capable, focused.

Behind closed doors there was screaming, shouting, and frequent bursts of anger, never a moment when the public perception translated into private peace. There was no way for me to prepare for the disruption that would carve itself onto my heart as abandonment.

By the time I was six years old, my mother, Shrenea, couldn't take it anymore and filed for divorce. She left our family home and took my sixteen-year-old sister, Christal, with her. Nine-year-old Sherri and I stayed in that three-story house with my father, who worked all the time. While other six-year-olds conjured up princesses and dinosaurs, I was laser-focused on survival. Sherri cooked my meals and made sure I did my homework. At age nine, she became the head of house and my guiding force.

But the day my mother loaded up the U-Haul van to take Sherri and me to Oklahoma, another disruption emerged in the form of bellowing wails that spilled from my father's throat when we left. The man whose anger had pummeled my early childhood, whose work-obsessed absence forced his children to be survivors, was now exposing a pain that seared my soul.

My father's anguish taught me that you can be deeply disruptive, yet still love deeply.

By age fourteen, my early disruption turned me into a fierce fighter and competitor. I landed my first after-school job at a grocery store in South Tulsa. As I bagged groceries, I turned on the charm. I enjoyed greeting people, helping them to their cars, and creating order in the aisles. That charm brought additional tips outside of my base pay, which helped my mother pay bills.

After graduating from the University of Tulsa, at some point I felt a heavy, gut-wrenching burden to serve the people in North Tulsa, whose lives had paralleled my own. I saw adults whose life choices and personal demons essentially left many rendered childlike. I saw kids who were forced to figure life out way too soon, with few resources, little to no food, and scant shelter. Without a parent's presence, guidance, and support, a child is robbed of their youthful elasticity, which I believe is the power to dream big and hope huge. You see, things are created twice, first in the mind, and then in reality. The Good Book tells us, "As [a man] thinketh in his heart, so is he" (Prov. 23:7). Whatever images are on the walls of our brains are often the very things that we attract into our lives.

That's how Oasis Fresh Market opened its doors on May 17, 2021. That vision yielded the first Black-owned full-service grocery store in North Tulsa in over fourteen years. What was once a food desert is now an oasis of possibility. We also launched a nonprofit called the Oasis Projects, which has wraparound services in the areas of housing, transportation, food, medical services, education, and workforce development. We are more than just groceries; we are equipping people for life!

I believe our model is what's needed in many of America's low-income, low-access communities. Grocery stores can stand as a sentinel for underserved, underresourced communities. They serve as meeting places that help disrupt the continued cycle of generational poverty rooted in too many communities across America, particularly in minority neighborhoods.

I vowed to disrupt that cycle in my own life. I'm now father to three beautiful daughters, aged seven, four, and two. My wife, Amber, and I often play a game with them where I ask them to close their eyes and tell us what they see. One daughter might say, "A pink unicorn pouring candy on the whole world." Another will say, "I see castles and dancing." And my youngest has said, "I see lions *roaring*!" Then I will say, "I see a refuge, a safe place, a shelter for millions of people living in underserved communities. A place where people are seen, safe, and heard. A place where everyone is welcome and respected."

As a father, I'm trying to disrupt their thinking. I'm trying to get them to see the hope of equity and justice. I want them to be just as happy to visualize a clean, safe, healthy neighborhood as they would be to see that pink unicorn. I want them to believe that both things are possible.

And that may be the most disruptive thought of all.

AARON "AJ" JOHNSON *is the founder and CEO of Oasis Fresh Market, the first full-service grocery store in fourteen years in North Tulsa, a predominantly Black neighborhood near Historic Greenwood's Black Wall Street District. Johnson also launched a nonprofit, the Oasis Projects, which provides wraparound services in the areas of housing stability, transportation solutions, food assistance, medical services, education, and workforce development. Johnson believes the Oasis model provides a blueprint for underserved communities by equipping people for every aspect of a healthy life.*

DR. ANITA PHILLIPS

As a therapist with an unorthodox approach, I love helping clients heal both one-on-one and in small groups. I was working as a professor training new counselors to do the same when I had a conversation with Bishop Jakes that truly disrupted me. Peering intensely over the top of his glasses, he leveled a challenge: "Why are you teaching twenty-five people at some college I never heard of, in some town I never heard of, when you have a message the world is dying without?" It was a pivotal moment.

I was already a disruptive thinker. As a graduate student I developed a new approach to therapy based on the idea that the Creator gave us enough information in Scripture and in nature to direct our scientific exploration of the human experience. I got a lot of resistance in certain academic circles, where I was told not to mix ideas—keep the spiritual out there, the biology over here, and the behavioral sciences there. For me, disruptive thinking was refusing to accept those divisions. I kick down walls in search of the truth.

When it comes to academics, the world is still a Tower of Babel; each profession is speaking a different language. I decided to become a professional polyglot—I speak public health; I speak social work; I speak neurobiology; I speak theology; I speak psychology. It's important to be able to speak languages across disciplines until you can teach a new language everyone can use together. Showing people that we're all saying the same thing, and giving them a lexicon to describe it, allows a seamless conversation. That seamless conversation exponentially increases our capacity to change lives.

So yes, I was already a disruptive thinker but, with one question, Bishop Jakes pushed me to a place I may have never gone on my own. He disrupted my beliefs about how "professional" information actually gets to the people who need it most. He inspired me to go from helping a handful of people at a time to touching lives en masse. I took a deep breath and big risk, and one year later, I was standing on stages that would allow my message to travel worldwide.

I've gone from working one-on-one in the therapy room to speaking and ministering to tens of thousands of people. In 2020 I started a podcast produced by the Woman Evolve Podcast Network called *In the Light*. It's a conversation at the intersection of faith, mental health, and culture. The response has been incredible; we had a million downloads in no time. People are hungry for the opportunity to have a real conversation that involves every part of who they are. I also wrote a book to help with that. Published in 2023, it's called *The Garden Within: Where the War with Your Emotions Ends and Your Most Powerful Life Begins*. Few mental health professionals get to catalyze this kind of social transformation. Disruptive thinking empowered me to do that.

DR. ANITA PHILLIPS *is a trauma therapist, author, and life coach. She has appeared as a subject matter expert on various media outlets, including ABC's* The Talk, *Jada Pinkett-Smith's* Red Table Talk, *Oprah's Live Your Best Life class, and the* Tamron Hall Show. *Dr. Anita is highly sought after for her unique ability to translate complex ideas into simple tools that empower people to transform their lives spiritually, emotionally, mentally, and physically.*

NOTES

2: WHY DO WE NEED DISRUPTIVE THINKING NOW?

1 Josh Bivens and Jori Kandra, "CEO Pay Has Skyrocketed 1,460% since 1978," Economic Policy Institute, October 4, 2022, https://www.epi.org/publication/ceo-pay-in-2021.

2 Phil Wahba, "CEO Pay Rose a Record 19% in 2021, while Employees Saw Paltry Raises," *Fortune*, April 1, 2022, https://fortune.com/2022/04/01/ceo-pay-rose-record-19-percent-2021.

3 Kimberly Amadeo, "What Does Income Inequality Look Like in the US?" April 20, 2022, The Balance, https://www.thebalancemoney.com/income-inequality-in-america-3306190.

4 Janelle Jones, "The Racial Wealth Gap," Economic Policy Institute, February 13, 2017, https://www.epi.org/blog/the-racial-wealth-gap-how-african-americans-have-been-shortchanged-out-of-the-materials-to-build-wealth.

5 Kimberly Amadeo, "Racial Wealth Gap in the United States," January 20, 2022, The Balance, https://www.thebalancemoney.com/racial-wealth-gap-in-united-states-4169678.

6 Ellora Derenoncourt, "Wealth of Two Nations: The U.S. Racial Wealth Gap, 1860–2020," Princeton Economics, May 2022, https://economics.princeton.edu/working-papers/wealth-of-two-nations-the-u-s-racial-wealth-gap-1860-2020.

7 Jennifer Ludden, "Here's One Reason Why America's Racial Wealth Gap Persists across Generations," NPR, August 13, 2022, https://www.npr.org/2022/08/13/1113814920/racial-wealth-gap-economic-inequality.

8 Ludden, "Here's One Reason."

9 "Many Rural Americans Are Still 'Left Behind,'" Institute for Research on Poverty, University of Wisconsin–Madison, https://www.irp.wisc.edu/resource/many-rural-americans-are -still-left-behind.

10 "Gap between Death Rates in Rural and Urban Areas Tripled during Past Two Decades," Medical XPress, June 8, 2021, https://medicalxpress.com/news/2021-06-gap-death-rural -urban-areas.html.

11 Aimee Picchi, "America's White Working Class Is the Smallest It Has Ever Been," CBS News, September 26, 2019, https:// www.cbsnews.com/news/americas-white-working-class-is-the -smallest-its-ever-been.

3: DISRUPTIVE PARTNERSHIPS

1 Peter Wagner and Wanda Bertram, "What Percent of the U.S. Is Incarcerated? (And Other Ways to Measure Mass Incarceration)," Prison Policy Initiative, January 16, 2020, https://www.prisonpolicy.org/blog/2020/01/16/percent -incarcerated.

2 Rakesh Kochhar and Stella Sechopoulos, "How the American Middle Class Has Changed in the Past Five Decades," Pew Research Center, April 20, 2022, https://www.pewresearch .org/fact-tank/2022/04/20/how-the-american-middle-class-has -changed-in-the-past-five-decades.

3 Margery Austin Turner, "More Evidence from Raj Chetty: Neighborhoods Matter for Economic Mobility," Urban Institute, May 4, 2015, https://www.urban.org/urban-wire /more-evidence-raj-chetty-neighborhoods-matter-economic -mobility.

5: WHY DISRUPT?

1 "How Long Does a Crack High Last?" Harmony Recovery Group, https://www.harmonyrecoverygroup.com/how-long -does-a-crack-high-last.

6: WHY IT'S SO DIFFICULT

1 Noel King, "A Brief History of How Racism Shaped Interstate Highways," NPR, April 7, 2021, https://www.npr.org/2021/04/07/984784455/a-brief-history-of-how-racism-shaped-interstate-highways.

2 "Mental Health Treatment among Adults: United States, 2019," National Center for Health Statistics, Centers for Disease Control and Prevention, September 2020, https://www.cdc.gov/nchs/products/databriefs/db380.htm.

11: PARENTING A DISRUPTER

1 "1 in 13 Children Taking Psychiatric Medication in US," Fox News, October 24, 2015, https://www.foxnews.com/health/1-in-13-children-taking-psychiatric-medication-in-us.